Three Coins in the Fountain

Falling In Love Through Faith, Family & Frequent Flyer Miles

CATHERINE TONDELLI
& FRANCESCA MAGGI

THREE COINS IN THE FOUNTAIN copyright ©2013

Printed in the United States of America. No part of this book may be used, reproduced, or distributed in digital form via the internet or otherwise without written permission, except in the case of brief quotations embodied in critical articles or reviews. For information and to request permissions, contact: Art&Media Communications POBox 7743 Bloomfield Hills, MI 48302 USA.

ISBN: 1461128145

ISBN-13: 978-1461128144

§ Dedication §

To mio caro amore Fausto, without whose unique way of seeing and putting things, this book would not have been possible
¯and¯
To my amazing mother, who, armed with an unwavering belief in love urged me to toss those three coins—and trust my heart.
All my determination, courage and faith I owe to you.
Oh – and, thanks Mom, for not stopping at kid no. 8…

Three hearts in a fountain / Each heart longing for its home /
There they lie in the fountain / Somewhere in the heart of Rome

Contents

❧

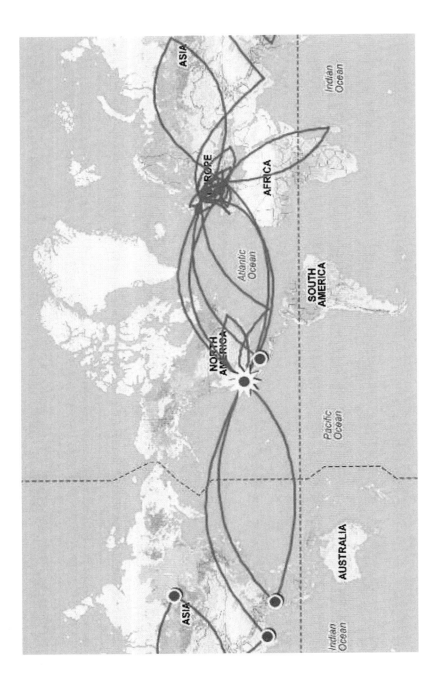

CHAPTER I

The Ides of March

It was March 15th, the *Ides of March*, that I found myself in the kitchen of my home in San Diego, California with my mother and my oldest sister, Renee. We were busy overseeing my ex-husband while he moved his stuff out of my house. Although we had officially annulled the marriage nearly a year before, he had asked if he could stay put until he could scrounge enough money together in order to move out. But as month followed month after month, I realized that the two of us, among our other differences, had completely divergent ideas of what constituted "just a little while." After about nine months and still seeing a men's shaving razor perched on my bathroom sink, I finally said, "Enough is enough!"—He had to collect his things and head out the door and out of my life—for good.

On this day that Caesar was assassinated, I couldn't help but feel it was a fitting ending to yet another disappointing love story;

one that this time I thought would have been different. Four years earlier, we had been falling in love, or so I believed. But the moment I put my faith in him, I began catching him in one white lie after another. In the end, he showed himself to be far from the successful, trustworthy man he had charmed me into believing he was. He had sold himself as a Rolls Royce but one good look under the hood and he was an old jalopy with a bright paint job. He turned out to be a fraud in more ways than one: I was caught out with my heart in pieces and holding what was left of our purse strings as well. He didn't even bat an eyelash when the bill collectors started to set their sights on me, gainfully employed with wages that could easily be garnished. Although my dream of living happily ever after was the collateral damage after four years of his sordid sorties, sussing out his true colors early on made it that much easier to quit the marital maneuvers and move on. Unlike my mom before me, I was glad I had found out sooner rather than later. Now, if only this princely toad would find another lily pad to occupy, warts and all.

My mother and my sister, the two people I counted on most my entire 39 years, were right there alongside me. Not only to provide moral support, but also to make sure that things didn't accidentally crawl out of the house while I wasn't looking. Sitting around my kitchen table, my eternally optimistic mom pointed out the window. "Look, Cathy—there's a bluebird sitting in your tree. He's flown here to bring you happiness." My very Irish-American mother always believed in signs from God, and this, most certainly, was one of them. If only.

While they kept their eyes on my ex, I was busy poring over maps of Italy. I had just won the top prize for sales in my company and would be officially lauded with a place in their lofty President's Club. The award was in recognition for being one of their top ad sales producers in the hotel field. Looking at my ne'er-do-well husband finally heading out the door for good, I figured in the end I really got a good deal. In the year I was freed up from the trials of trying to carry on a healthy relationship with him, I spent surpassing all of our sales targets. As always, I had proved myself once again to be a failure in love, but flourishing at work.

President's Club members would be rewarded with a first-class trip for two to Venice, all expenses paid. The trip included one week at the luxurious five-star *Hotel Danieli*, located right off the beautiful and bustling *Piazza San Marco*—Saint Mark's Square, private dinners in Venetian palaces, *gondola* trips, the works. With an ex-husband going out the door and no one special in my life to replace him, I decided to take my mother along as my companion. Certainly, she was an easy travelling partner who was fun, cultured and who, even after raising eleven kids, still had vast reserves of energy to keep up with me, an indefatigable social butterfly. Besides, she had dreamed of Italy almost her whole life. How could I not bring her along? Moreover, if it hadn't been for my mom, I most likely would never have gotten where I was today. I was truly looking forward to sharing with her what I'm sure would turn out to be a trip of a lifetime. I had no doubt about it: It was Mary Lee who deserved a stint in the President's Club after all the trials and tribulations she had gone through in her life. And even though she lived quite modestly, I was pretty certain she'd be up for a lap of luxury as a guest in the Venetian lagoon.

Making our plans, we decided that a single week in Italy would not be nearly enough. It was her first trip to Italy, and my mom wanted to see Rome and Florence as well. As she always put it in her ever- endearing way, "Honey, I can't *die* until I have laid my eyes on Rome!" So there we were, studying guidebooks and going over our itinerary for our two-week holiday to *Bell' Italia*. We were determined to make the most of it.

All the President's Women

Although I was an inveterate traveler, combing most of the United States in nearly twenty years of work, my mom never had the opportunity to see as much of the world as she had wanted. Even after having left a teaching job to work for American Airlines, she still didn't burn up the miles like the rest of us. Retired to Hawaii, she used her travel perks to pay a visit to one child or another. She ultimately came out to California to be closer to me and some of my siblings and to enjoy those of her grandchildren who lived out west. Although of Irish descent, she had gone ahead and married my dad, an Italian-American, and they had planned to go to Italy for as long as I could remember. He went there, all right—accompanied by his new wife—and twelfth child. Although this trip may have brought up pangs of nostalgia for what hadn't been, Mary Lee was ready and raring to go.

Of course. I knew my mom would be unflappable. Raising eleven kids would certainly make managing hours of air travel, plane changes and time zones a breeze by comparison. It wasn't enough to have brought up the lot of us, but trying at the same time to teach inner city school kids mathematics day in and day out was probably no picnic in the park, either. It was the 1950s and my mom had three boys before finally giving birth to a baby girl, Renee. Then seven more kids followed, including a set of twins of which I was one half. Growing up in Chicago, it seemed that my mom was on a first-name basis with the local police department. The three oldest boys were quite a handful, always finding trouble if trouble didn't seek them out first. While we girls almost never gave her any flak, the boys with my eldest brother Joe the uncontested leader of the pack, truly put her to the test. Mary Lee usually laughed it all off while running to the jail to post bond, my father screaming after her, "Leave 'em in there! It'll teach 'em a lesson!" But she would always bail them out and try to talk some reason back into them on the way home, before heading into the house to try and temper my dad. It never worked. Needless to say, I grew up rest assured that my brothers would always have my back.

Landing at *Marco Polo Airport,* neither of us was quite prepared for the overwhelming emotion of seeing Venice in all her magnificence from afar. Venice, be it for the very first time or for a thousand times thereafter, always takes your breath away. Whoever made the statement, *"See Naples then die,"* had clearly never set foot in *La Serenissima* Republic of Venice. Upon clearing customs, we were met by private boat and literally swept away for our fantasy week holiday amidst the splendid palaces and tiny footbridges that tied all the streets together like a complicated latticework in 3D. My mom and I took turns peeking our heads out of the wooden boat to feel the cool April air as we approached the scattering of islets that make up the whole of the Venetian lagoon. Venturing to Venice by boat, you can't help but feel your heart start to quicken. Boats of every size and shape coming and going all around you make you stop to think of the countless travellers and traders that have passed through this city of palaces, courtyards, churches and docks. From the sea, Venice has a ghostlike presence; its haze muffling the millions of voices and stories that have gone before. Once upon the canals, you see surreal Venice in an entirely different light. Regardless, from any perspective, Venice always feels more like a movie set than an actual town.

In our short ride across the bay, I couldn't help but think what story Venice would unveil for me going forward. Arriving in this magical city, I was finally on my own, embarking on a new life ahead. I took one look back from the boat to ponder everything I had left in my wake. I vowed that this would be the start of a new dawn on my new, single and sensible life. Upon our approach, we caught our first glimpse of the only skyscraper in Venice: the pointed brick bell tower perched on Saint Mark's Square. Venice seemed like the perfect fairytale setting in which to leave behind the dreary disappointments that seemed to beset me back home. I had achieved great success and recognition in my career, but that same success never seemed to transfer into my personal life. I was quite convinced that I was the perfect embodiment of a modern update to that old yarn, *"Lucky at cards, unlucky in love."* But for career women like me, a more accurate description would be, *"Lucky at work, unlucky in love."* As I took in the sights off the stunning Grand Canal, I imagined that this was simply the hand I had been dealt. Little did I know just how soon that deck would be shuffled and the odds turned in my favor.

Our boat pulled right up from the Grand Canal to the front of our hotel. The *Hotel Danieli* was reputedly one of the finest hotels in the entire Venetian lagoon. The boat slowed down, pulling up to their private dock decked out with those whimsical candy-striped mooring poles. Their dignified doormen quickly helped us out of the boat before grabbing our cases and guiding us down the tiny alley and into the hotel. Upon entering, we were offered a sparkling welcome *Bellini* in their opulent Venetian Gothic reception hall before being escorted up to our room. Once inside, our jaws literally dropped from the breathtaking view from our window overlooking the canals. From there, we could see the lovely white Bridge of Sighs that I had read about in my guidebook. Prisoners of the past may have breathed a sigh of longing at their last gaze upon Venice before heading to a life in prison, but I took a look at the bridge and heaved a great sigh of relief; comfortable with the knowledge that my marriage was finally over and that I would be starting anew.

We took turns taking baths and getting ready for the first night's reception and dinner at the *Danieli*. Right on time, we arrived in the dining room of this glorious historic hotel, practically speechless underneath the beauty of the vast ceiling covered in frescoes, by the lavish paintings decorating the walls, and by the furnishings from long ago and far away. The porter had told us that this had once been the private home of an important Doge of Venice—a sort of Town Mayor—and that we were staying in the original part of his home, built back in the 12th century.

At dinner, everyone in the President's Club introduced their spouses or partners. *"This is my wife Susan…" "My husband Jim…"* At my turn, I was unbelievably proud to introduce my mom, Mary Lee. After my father had walked out on the family, we never truly understood just how much she had had to struggle to raise the five of us still at home on her paltry teacher's salary. To this day, I am incapable of calculating how she managed with enough to cover the rent and grocery bills just to keep us going for the month. It was even more difficult to comprehend how, through it all, she remained unwavering in her love, and unrelenting in her joy for giving. Later that evening, while enjoying drinks up on the *Danieli* roof terrace, we both stood there in blissful silence, taking in the spectacular view of all of Saint Mark's Square, its church topped with four rearing horses, and the *Basilica of Santa Maria della Salute* just across the Grand Canal. I had to pinch myself to feel just how far the two of us had come.

Mary Lee was absolutely overjoyed with a night of being fêted in this over-the-top luxurious Italian way. Although through the years we had had many beautiful times together as a family, I was glowing at the sight of my mom surrounded by so much elegance and so many warm faces. It was a far cry from the time my sisters and I had orchestrated a party in her honor back in our tiny Chicago apartment after my dad had left home. She was feeling quite downbeat at the prospect of hitting the milestone of 50, especially after my dad had decided to trade in his ol' jalopy for a newer model.

We kids decided to throw a surprise party for her. We phoned all her friends and decorated our dismal apartment as festively as possible. We scrabbled together all our money to buy her a birthday cake. Even still, we could only get one from Heinemann's reject bakery shop; the final resting place for unsold cakes or for those that weren't in any condition to be on display in the first place. We paid eight dollars for a huge butter cream sheet cake, enough to feed 20 people. With the rest, we bought cheese and crackers and cheap champagne. That evening, my mom walked through the door after a long day at work. In her hand was a tiny cake she had bought for herself. Upon laying eyes on all of us gathered there screaming out *"Surprise!"* she nearly keeled right over. To this day she says it was one of the most wonderful birthdays she had ever had.

Heading back to our room at this exquisite Venetian *palazzo* right on the canal, I could tell that, though the years were showing in her sweet 75-year old face, there was no denying the joy and happiness of a lifetime of memories in her beautiful, green Irish eyes.

CHAPTER II

~⌒~

A (few) Rooms with a View

We awoke the next morning to the sound of pigeons cooing in Saint Mark's Square. Outside our window and coming off the canal, we also heard the distinct sound of Italian arias being sung right underneath our window; emanating from gondoliers trying to entice customers. As I looked out our window, one of them yelled up, "*Buongiorno Signorina—How would you like a tour with one of the most handsome gondoliers in Venice?*" "No thanks!" I called out, "My mom and I have a full day ahead of us, but thanks anyway!" My company had scheduled a tour guide to take us all around to some of the more important Venetian sights. I could tell it was going to be an amazing day.

That evening, we were taken by private boat over to Venice's beach area, the *Lido*. There, we would be fêted again at the famous *Grand Hotel Excelsior* with a sumptuous five-course dinner and an awards ceremony. This was the same venue where they give out the

Golden Lion awards at the annual Venice Film Festival. My mom recalled that it was also the very same hotel where the big stars of her day, such as Errol Flynn, Barbara Hutton and Elizabeth Taylor, had stayed. As I crossed the stage to accept my Baccarat crystal for stellar sales, I could tell Mary Lee was beaming with pride. In her eyes, I might as well have just won the Oscar. The evening carried on well into the night with sublime music and dancing, lively chatter and general joviality. We were having so much fun that I surprised everyone in our group by getting up and playing trumpet with the orchestra! The (all-male) Italian band members were left speechless, not to mention my coworkers.

Mary Lee's dream trip to
Italy-Unforgettable for both of us

My dad had been a jazz musician, and I had been surrounded by music my entire life. I had taken up the trumpet when I was still in grade school, practicing with all my heart and hoping to become as good as he one day; persevering long after my dad had left home. For me, those notes blasting out into the ether are what kept me tied to my ghost of a father. He left us shortly after my twin sister and I turned thirteen. He had simply up and left without as much as a goodbye to start a whole new life—one without eleven urchins to care for nor care about. Delivering the news over dinner, my mom had flatly made the pronouncement that my dad had left and would not be coming back. Ever. He proved to be a seriously 'deadbeat dad,' never living up to his responsibilities—namely the lot of us left behind. In fact, he left us high and dry, providing no alimony nor child support. Incredibly, he managed to get a 25-year, 11-child marriage annulled. But even more outrageously, he spawned two more offspring; a last ditch effort to convince himself that he'd "get it right the next time." For a girl just heading into adolescence, this dramatic chain of events unleashed in under 18 months came as quite a shock to the system.

Unbeknownst to me, abandonment by my dad signified that I would embark on a lifetime quest to gain his approval. But even before then, I had tried so very hard to stand out in his eyes; to stand out in the crowd that was all my siblings. I proved to be quite adept at the trumpet, and longed for my musician father to praise my budding talent. Instead, he sent me out of the house to practice in the garage— just so he wouldn't dare be disturbed. Even during the harsh Chicago winters, there I'd be, outside practicing with gloves on. A few years later, I was selected as one of five high school students to play with the Chicago Symphony Orchestra. The piece was *The Pines of Rome* written by Italian composer, Ottorino Respighi. I invited my dad to the concert, hoping beyond hope that he'd be impressed with my performance. It would be my chance to shine and finally win him over. True to form, he never even bothered to show up for the concert that night.

After my *Grand Hotel* debut, we danced until the last private speedboat whisked us hardcore partiers back to *Piazza San Marco* and back to the *Danieli*. It had been an unforgettable evening.

11

Venetian Days & Nights

The next few days were spent with mornings on organized tours guiding us through St Mark's Basilica, into the Doge's Palace and up and over the *Rialto Bridge*. Afternoons we were left to roam by ourselves which we filled strolling through the labyrinth of alleyways on a mission to buy masks, jewelry and stationery on fine, handmade paper. One afternoon, we took a water taxi to the small island of *Burano* so my mom could pick up some of its famous lace and I could see its colorfully painted homes. While on the islet of *Murano*, a cute Italian guy tried picking me up, even with my mother right nearby. He was relentless in his persuasion, and, although I feigned disinterest, I had to admit it sure felt great to have a 'skirt chaser' look my way. In the USA, you'd practically have to light yourself on fire in order for a guy to show that kind of unyielding pursuit. Say what you will about Italian men, but they certainly put the 'R' into romance. Another afternoon we headed over to see Venice's *La Fenice Opera House*. Appropriately named, this 'Phoenix' had burnt down to the ground more than once, only to be built right back again in all its original splendor. I wondered if I could manage to do the same with my own life. Certainly, it would not be the first time.

Although I don't actually recall this episode, engraved in the Tondelli family lore is the time when our own home had burnt down to the ground. I was still a toddler when one of my older brothers decided to try out a cigarette that a friend had given him. He saved it until the day my mother and father had a dinner engagement, and he'd be at home with my eldest brother babysitting the rest of us. He must have waited 'til we all went to bed, because by the time he decided to cop a smoke, it was late. But no sooner had he lit up than he heard my parents' Oldsmobile pull up in the driveway. Terrified at getting found out, he skittishly stashed the cigarette under the seat of our living room couch, tore up the stairs and jumped into bed. About two hours later our entire house was up in smoke. And while we all managed to get out in time before it burned down completely, it was the aftermath that proved to be the truly difficult hurdle. We had to be dispersed to relatives, friends or to whatever charitable soul would deign to take in parts of our clan indefinitely; or at least until we found another house to move into. For us kids, however, living for a time with families with fewer kids gave us a taste of the good life: we were treated to real milk, meat dishes, and even luscious ice cream. As the weeks wore on, going back home even to a brand new apartment and even as a united front just did not hold the same allure as our fantasy food fests we'd be leaving behind.

Later on, it would be my turn to light the house on fire a second time. My sister Andrea was teaching me to light matches down in the basement. She would light them, blow them out and then toss them in the trash. After she had left the room, I decided to try my hand; only this time, I forgot to blow it out first before tossing the burning match away. Seeing smoke rising up from the trashcan, I ran and hid. The entire basement went up in flames, including the brand new pool table my father had just finished paying off. After the fire had finally been put out, both my sister and I got ours. Although my backside smarted for days, at least we all still had our roof over our heads.

Our last night in Venice, we were taken by gondola to a masquerade ball. It was held inside the 15th century *Palazzo Pisani Moretta*. Perched at one of the most bewitching junctures right on the Grand Canal, this palace houses some of the finest works of 18th century Venetian artists ever to be found. We entered the building and were taken aback by its majestic stairway. Upstairs, we were treated to yet another candlelight dinner served beneath frescoes by Tiepolo. Musicians dressed in Baroque costumes serenaded us the entire evening. It would be nearly impossible to break the enchantment and leave this spellbinding place that was *Venezia*.

Under the Tuscan Sun

While planning our trip around the kitchen table, my mom had insisted she set foot in Rome, the *Città Eterna*, the *Eternal City*. It had been 20 years since I had been there with my twin sister, so without skipping a beat, I said I would absolutely be game to go with her. But first, we'd make a stop along the way through Florence.

Our Venetian Escorts

We spent two days in the beguiling red-roofed city, eating and walking our way across *Piazza Duomo* and its Baptistery, in and out of dozens of churches (so many we lost count), over the charming *Ponte Vecchio*, and up inside the *Pitti Palace*. We stood for hours in line like a pair of Rolling Stones groupies just to catch a glimpse of a Florentine rock star: Botticelli's *Primavera* at the *Uffizi Gallery*. We got sidetracked roaming the stalls at a flea market, costing us all our spare change and our lunch at a *ristorante*. We found out the hard way that in Italy, mealtimes are highly stringent and you won't be served more than snacks at a coffee bar if you aren't seated and ready to order well before the stroke of 2 o'clock. Making the most of it, we grabbed a sandwich and a *gelato* and had ourselves a picnic in the *Piazza della Signoria*, graced by the sinuous statue of Michelangelo's *David*. Visiting the *Accademia Gallery* later that afternoon, we discovered that the statue we had seen outdoors was merely a copy; the splendid original protected from bird 'baths' and the elements was the magnificent centerpiece of the entire gallery. It was all the more astonishing to learn that Michelangelo had crafted his young *David* when he, himself, was only 26 years old. Between the two, I couldn't decide who was the true hero of this story, David or Michelangelo. We stood there admiring the beautiful features cast in a single block of marble before moving on to see Botticelli's *Madonna and Child* and the plaster cast for Giambologna's *Rape of the Sabines*.

Our final day in Florence was spent at the *Pitti Palace* and the surrounding park behind it, the *Boboli Gardens*. It was an unusually warm day, so we spent the afternoon getting lost within the labyrinth of hedges cut in every shape and size. We strolled around the pools and grottoes and past dozens of statues adorning all of the walkways. Tired out from the hilly walk, we finally decided to take a breather and just sit down and relax and enjoy the outstanding bird's eye view of Florence just below us, delighting in the perfume from the blossoming spring flowers. I closed my eyes thinking about the beauty of the Florentines and their Renaissance. Out on this great lawn, it brought to mind the times when the weather was nice, all us kids would play 'statue' out on our patch of a lawn in Chicago. One of us would be the buyer who would come into the store to select a statue. The rest of us had to create different poses that might pique the buyer's interest. We were a cast of frozen ballerinas, soldiers, opera singers. The dealer would set the scene in motion, showing off the collection. On cue, each statue would get a chance to demonstrate his or her abilities to the collector. The buyer would then select their favorite. Our makeshift masterpiece marketplace would go on for hours on end. We were always fortunate to have enough players around for just about any game and also the ones that didn't cost money.

The next morning, we decided to have one last view of the *Arno* river off the *Ponte Vecchio* before heading to the train station. The bridge is lined on both sides by gold jewelers. Years earlier, my brother Jimmy had bought my mom a garnet ring from Florence, but it had gone lost. Standing there on the exquisite bridge, she told me that she wanted to buy a similar one to replace it. In no time at all, Mary Lee was the proud owner of a lovely garnet ring set in 18 kt gold. She was in seventh heaven. She practically skipped all the way to the *Santa Maria Novella* train station. And in just three short hours, her dream of Rome would also become reality.

Three Coins in the Fountain

We would be spending only three days in Rome, so we were determined to pack in all of the sights that we possibly could. We checked into an adorable *pensione*, a small family-run inn located right on the famed *Via Veneto*. With its luxury hotels and outdoor cafés lining the streets, it didn't appear to have lost any of its splendor from the time it was made famous by Federico Fellini and his *Dolce Vita*. Arriving in Rome was like seeing an old friend and oh, how I had missed her…But just like an old friend, Rome appeared vastly different to me than when I had seen her a full two decades earlier. Back then I had stayed nearer to Vatican City. Here in this part of Rome, with its elegant palaces morphed into luxury hotels, its wide boulevards and spacious outdoor restaurants, the city seemed to me like a totally different place altogether. Although the center of Rome is quite small, it's like an oversized patchwork; each section with its own distinct feel, its unique history, its very own spice cabinet full of smells and colors, and all mixed in with a singular architectural style from the period that the neighborhood came to be.

Our first night out in Rome, we walked down the *Via Veneto* toward the center of Rome. We sat down to an absolutely divine dinner of *cannelloni* and *lasagna*, both prepared like God, if he were a master Italian chef, intended them to be. While we wined and dined, we recounted our day's events. It was all picture perfect; until, of course, it came time for our bill. I noticed an item that read *coperto 4,000 lire* each. I immediately flagged down the owner to tell him that we didn't order anything called *coperto* and that we had no intention to pay for it. An argument ensued, which I decidedly lost in the end. We ended up paying the whole bill *8,000 lire coperto* charge and all. It would be only much later that I would discover that this was a common practice in Italy; levying a 'table charge' for anyone who sat down to simply enjoy a meal. In our heated discussion and between his English and my pigeon Italian, I was also able to discern that we were told to leave and to never come back.

The scene at the restaurant somewhat dampened our spirits, but heading back to our hotel we noticed a sign for the *Trevi Fountain*. Although we had planned on going the next day, I didn't want to end our first day in glorious Rome on such a crummy note. So I said to my mom, "Let's just go tonight instead of tomorrow—I'm sure the fountain will look positively gorgeous at night. It will be totally illuminated and I read it's just been cleaned for the Vatican Jubilee. I'm sure it'll be such a terrific treat!"

I felt very much at home in Rome, wandering through the small, narrow streets, stopping in the small shops of yesteryear, and getting lost in the maze of her churches, palaces, *piazzas* and pizzerias. They say that your memory is always jogged by smell. Meandering along the old city streets, those familiar scents brought the Rome I remembered back in full, living color. I could tell the corner pizzerias a full block away; places where they sell a medley of unbelievably delicious pizza-by-the-slice. They display their pies heaped with toppings from zucchini and anchovies to tuna fish with mozzarella and basil, and they use scissors to cut precisely how much you want. Everywhere we went, my head would fill with the aroma of *espresso* being brewed in the ubiquitous coffee bars. And then there were the endless lines for *gelato* on a hot spring day.

For me, *gelato* was the very best, extra-special, über-scrumptious treat that money could buy. Growing up, ice cream was served only on very special occasions, and even then, there was barely enough to go around. My dad kept his own personal stock of *31 Flavors* chocolate-chip ice cream under lock and key, buried in the freezer in our basement. One fine day, my brother Tony figured out how to pick the lock. From that day forward, we would take turns sneaking downstairs, one by one, spoon in hand. We would very carefully dig into the 3-gallon barrel of ice cream to our heart's delight. We kept this up for ages. But our gluttonous escapades came to an end one day when we heard adult footsteps coming down the basement stairs. We quickly threw our spoons into the bin and slammed the freezer door shut. The next day, our gig was up when my mother found eight giant spoons frozen into the ice cream bin.

We stopped at a *gelateria* for a delicious ice cream cone piled high with three flavors, or *tre gusti*. We got to choose from a virtual rainbow of ice cream and sorbet displayed in tidy rows of lusciousness behind huge glass cases. Cones in hand, we decided to sit down right in front of the riotous spectacle that was the *Trevi Fountain* and revel in the dizzying splendor of its winged horses hurtling toward us, the hordes of people milling about, the shoots of water pouring from all sides. Newly cleaned, the stark white figures from the fountain appeared like nothing I had ever seen before. It was vastly different from the first time I had seen it over 20 years prior; she had shed her ashen coat and was absolutely sparkling under the lights of her bright, new, shiny façade.

As I stood there in my revelry, my mother blurted out right out of nowhere, "Right, Cathy. It's time that you make a wish for a nice man to come into your life. Here's three coins. Now go ahead and make your wish!" Slightly amused, but caught up in the spirit of the moment, I took them from her hand, turned around, and tossed them in…One, two, three…*Via!!!* No sooner had I launched them in the air than I heard a sweet Italian voice saying, "*Eeffa you wanta your wish to comb true, you avv to trow the coins witah your layft (h)and as eet's closer to your (h)art…*" "Wow!" I thought, "Boy, this fountain works fast!" I thanked the guy for his advice, telling him I would give it another go. Certainly, it wouldn't hurt to have another chance at love. "This time," I promised, "I'll throw the three coins in with my left hand."

"*No,*" he said. "*You know de meaning of da tree coins?*" he asked, leaving out the unpronounceable 'th', I observed. Actually, I was completely clueless as to why we had to throw three coins—in fact, the only thing that came to mind was Frank Sinatra crooning about three coins, not two, in the fountain. Taking my faltering for a certain request for a reply, the guy offered up his explanation. "*Da first coin, you find your love in Rome, da second coin, you return to Rome and the t(h)ird coin, you marry in Rome.*" Mary Lee, by this time clearly charmed by this stranger, started to giggle and the man

18

introduced himself as Fausto. Instantly, my mom, quick to make the most of her good fortune of finally meeting a local, began plying him with questions on what we should see and do in Rome. And even more importantly, where she should go to buy good leather shoes—naturally, at a bargain. For her, this chance meeting with a bona fide, authentic Italian was a GMC—God-Manufactured Coincidence, as she loved to call it. A GMC—when two seemingly unrelated events conspire to bring good fortune to those involved. In my opinion, these Italian men popping up out of nowhere like mushrooms were more like God-Manufactured Inconveniences.

Putting his best Italian foot forward, Fausto suggested politely that she buy her shoes in America where they would definitely be cheaper. But if she really wanted a pair of fine Italian shoes, he suggested she try the *Via Nazionale*. The two of them carried on their animated conversation that seemed to go on for all eternity. "Eternal City, all right," I thought to myself. Standing there, as mute as one of the Madonna statues perched on a corner nearby, I figured I must have thrown the coins seriously the wrong way. It didn't help that both my mom and Fausto soon discovered they were both airline people. Fausto worked for Alitalia and Mary Lee had recently retired from American Airlines. I always find that no matter where you are, airline people always seem to share an uncommon bond as if they were part of a grand, global fraternity and as such, capable of speaking to each other for donkey years. Between the argument with the restaurateur and now this joker, I couldn't wait to get out of there and back to the private confines of our charming *pensione.*

While plotting to find the right moment to make a subtle exit, I heard our quite dashing Fausto say, in all seriousness, that he was waiting for two gentleman friends from Verona. I cracked a smile. He told us that his two friends were both flight attendants and seeing that their flight was late into Rome, he had at least one hour available that he could devote to us. Well, that sealed the deal for me. Here he was, this good looking, well-coifed man, alone on a Saturday night waiting for two male flight attendants…Hmmm… it didn't take long for me to deduct that he was surely gay. And if that were the case, those coins had backfired more than ever.

19

Fausto ventured further to ask if we were interested in taking a quick walk around to some of the nearby historical sites. If so, he would be happy to be our guide. Before I could utter a word and politely decline the invitation, Mary Lee quickly chimed in for the two of us, saying that would be just lovely. I just as quickly shot over a piercing look to let her know that it would have been totally nice if she had consulted with me first before making her snap decision on my behalf. Incredibly, she added that the only problem was that she really couldn't walk as much as a single step further this evening, since we had been going since 8:00 that morning.

She pressed on, just for good measure, saying that since having been hit by a car some twenty years prior, she still had problems standing for long periods of time. As if my mom hadn't had it rough enough: while waiting for a bus on Michigan Avenue in downtown Chicago, a woman lost control of her car and ran into the crowd of people waiting there—my mother happened to be standing at the wrong place at the wrong time. And in my opinion, here she was again: wrong place, wrong time. I was relieved to know that by virtue of her explanation we had just dodged a bullet. But before I could count my blessings, right out of the blue the next thing I heard was, "*No problema—I go anda pickupa my car and I take you on my Rome-by-Night tour.*" I couldn't believe my ears. There was Mary Lee, once again beaming that that would be just super. Before I could even register on just what escapade my mother had thrown us into with this gay Italian guy, I heard Fausto saying, "*Andiamo! Let's go.*" Suddenly, I found myself winding our way through the crowds, trying not to lose sight of Fausto as he darted in and out of people and over to his car.

CHAPTER III

~⌒~

Roman Holiday

What was *Rome-by-Night* anyway? Fausto told us to wait for him on the thoroughfare and he'd be there in a heartbeat to retrieve us. I couldn't comprehend why my mother had placed so much trust in this perfect Italian stranger that we had met just 15 minutes earlier. For all either of us knew, he could be preparing to take us down a dark alley, steal all our valuables and we'd never be heard from again. I clutched my handbag a bit tighter as I envisioned the morning's headlines. Great. But I, for one, couldn't open my mouth. Seeing that we had just left behind my flaky ex-husband, I certainly wasn't the best judge of character, that was for sure. Looking back, in fact, it seemed nearly everyone I had picked out turned out to be the wrong kind of guy. And frankly, my mom, having fallen head-over-heels for the fun-loving lout that my dad turned out to be, well, she wasn't much of a prize fisherman either went it came to reeling in the good catch. Nonetheless, I would have to go with my mom's judgment. "Honey, I just have this gut feeling that he's a really nice man. And, besides, what have we got to lose?"

Still, I couldn't help raise my objections, loud and clear: "What if he picks us up in one of those tiny cars, or worse, a *Vespa* motor scooter that all three of us will have to sit on?!" My mom just rolled her eyes and kept lookout for Fausto, her new best friend. A few minutes later, at the sound of brakes screeching, we laid eyes on Fausto who at that moment was pulling straight up and over the curb right to where we were waiting. To prove to me how silly I had sounded, my mom said, "And look! He even has a *four-door* car! I *knew* he was a nice man!" "Terrific," I thought to myself, "now men pass muster by the number of car doors they're sporting." My mom insisted that I sit in the front seat, so we all clambered in and set off on our way to see *Rome-by-Night*. First stop: The Roman Forum. Again, with what I would come to regard as typical Italian style, Fausto pulled his car right up on the sidewalk, parking it as close as a motor vehicle could get to the Temple of Saturn. My mom and I exchanged looks of utter disbelief. We didn't quite know what to make of it. We could tell that he was enthusiastic but this was ridiculous. Without so much as a word, Fausto simply got out of the car and shut the door. Determining that this was a case of 'doing as the Romans do,' we followed suit.

Leave it to the Italians to go one better than my mother's traditional tactic of finding a perfect parking spot. Her tried and true method was praying to St Anthony, the saint called upon to find anything and everything. Whenever we were out with my mom, she would engage him as her personal parking valet. Back at home she would always count on his powers to bring to light anything that went lost around the house. And with eleven kids, she pretty much had a hotline straight up to the heavens. I knew the prayer by heart:

"Saint Anthony, perfect imitator of Jesus, who received from God the special power of restoring lost things, grant that I may find (the keys, a parking spot, etc., etc.) which has been lost and needs to be found..."

Paying no attention to our bewilderment over his makeshift parking place, Fausto casually proceeded to give us his *Reader's Digest* version of the Roman Forum. He concluded his soliloquy by stating quite emphatically how important the Forum and all of Ancient Rome, really, was to all mankind. Naturally, the implication was, how extraordinary the Romans were for managing to preserve the ruins right up 'til today. Unfortunately for Fausto, much of his explanation fell on deaf ears. I could tell my mother had spent the entire time only half-listening, totally preoccupied over his Italian parking job rather than concentrating on the vast significance of the Roman Empire. Finally voicing her concerns, she asked him straight out if it was truly all right to leave his car like that right up on the sidewalk. Fausto took one look at her, smiled widely and said, *"Tis ees Roma, Mary Lee, not New York..."* And with this, our gracious Roman tour guide turned back to the broken columns of the Forum lit up at night with the moon shining brightly above the Colosseum. I certainly couldn't have agreed more.

Back inside the car, we headed up the *Via dei Fori Imperiali*, the wide avenue with the monumental Colosseum filling the entire view in the distance. *"You see, thee Colosseum, she isa not ah so hellteey... Can you see all da holes in her? She is a verry sick lady...During the war they took out all her metal to use for da vaypones...and before then, some of the metal Bernini had used to make the great baldacchino of Saint Peters. Did you know dis?"* For the second time in almost as many minutes, my mom and I swapped puzzled looks. Finally, it dawned on us that he meant 'weapons,' not *vaypones*. But we only figured out what the great *baldacchino* was the next day, when we were inside St Peter's Basilica. It was the marvelous bronze canopy with its candy cane columns reaching up to the heavens, and supposedly housing the 'throne' of St Peter himself. We didn't know what the bronze must have looked like on the Colosseum, but what Bernini did with it was truly remarkable.

Our next stop was over on the *Quirinale Hill*, one of the seven hills of Rome, and onto the expansive *piazza* stretching out in front of a huge palace situated there. As he unabashedly parked his car right in front of the immense fountain of horses in its square, Fausto informed us that his president lived inside the *Quirinale*

Palace just in front of us. I was shocked that anyone could get that close to what was essentially the Italians' White House; let alone park a car right out front as if stopping in to ask to borrow a cup of sugar. Just as this thought crossed my mind, a policeman came up to our car and told Fausto he couldn't leave it there. But instead of backing down instantly and scooting off to—oh, I don't know, park in a perfectly legal spot, Fausto in response, told me to hand the policeman my passport.

Caught up in the whirlwind frenzy of motion that was Fausto, I don't know why, but I found myself reaching in my handbag and pulling out my American passport. Demonstrating it to the policeman, Fausto later told us that he said, *"I am transporting these Americans to their (h)otel. Don't you see, the elder woman in my car, she cannot walk. They have travelled from California to see our Casa Bianca* (White House) *and you don't want to disappoint them do you?"* I was dumbstruck by the sheer audacity. I couldn't help but think he was going to get us all arrested, talking back to a policeman and within earshot of the president of the country. Visions of *One Flew Over the Cuckoo's Nest* went through my head.

But even I had to admit, I quite enjoyed Fausto's chutzpah. He wasn't afraid to take chances and moreover, I would soon discover, like every red-blooded Roman, to talk his way out of any sticky situation. The police officer took one look in the car and then, flashing a big smile, gestured to us that it was okay to step out of the car and have a look around. My mom and I were giddy with delight. The view over all of Rome from this terrace vantage point was truly awesome. Even in the darkness, there was nothing but terracotta rooftops and church towers for as far as the eye could see. As for Italy's presidential palace, Fausto, in his matter-of-fact way of dispensing odd information, informed us that it was of little import who, exactly, the president happened to be. Italian presidents were simply figureheads and not the head honcho. I couldn't believe that an Italian citizen would be giving such a blasphemous commentary; right on the front porch of their very own White House, no less. Fausto went on to tell us that in terms of governing, it was the prime minister who really pulled the political strings. Well, that explained the reason for people milling about the *piazza* there, and right in full view of the palace guards.

24

Hearing him speak, Fausto struck me as the quintessential Roman—it was clear he was very proud of his *Bella Roma*. I was starting to even warm up to him. He was quite knowledgeable and witty, and moreover, he had Pat Metheny's *Passage to Paradise* CD playing in his car, which to this day is still one of my favorite albums. Taking a cue from my Irish mom, I thought that it was another sure sign from God. Perhaps this chance encounter wasn't so freaky after all. He was certainly charming enough, I thought, and very handsome besides. He also was so easy to talk to, having been blessed of course, with that very Italian gift of gab. Even though he might be gay, I felt oddly comfortable with this even odder Roman. Truth be told, I couldn't remember the last time I had laughed so much with any man. It may not be a passage to paradise, but for the first time in a long while, in the company of this dashing *bon vivant*, at least I felt I wasn't in purgatory.

At night's end, we finally pulled up to our hotel. As we got out to leave, Fausto asked how he could contact me again. I handed him my business card. Scrutinizing it, he was shocked to read my last name. *"Whatda??! But your surname ees Eetalian why ees it you cannot speak even a word?!"* For the first time the entire evening, it was his turn to be dumbfounded. He then seized the opportunity to ask in his genteel manner if he could offer us a nightcap of *limoncello* or an after-dinner drink. By this time, it was clear he no longer cared about meeting up with his two friends. As for me, I was seriously bummed out that our tour had to end so soon. Seeing us hesitate a moment, he tried upping the ante: *"How would you like to see Piazza San Pietro—St Peter's Square—all leet up at night?"*

My mom politely demurred, saying she was tired and needed to get to bed. Encouraging me to go ahead and go out without her, I could tell she was saying this partly because she had seen a flicker of electricity between us. She left so the two of us could spend some time alone and maybe get to know each other a little bit better. With my mother upstairs in bed, off we went to a small bar behind *Piazza Navona*, called Jonathan's Angels. Fausto ordered two *limoncello*s while regaling me with stories about his life; all delivered in almost perfect English coupled with his very cute Italian accent. He told me all about his family, his two brothers and their families. He also informed me as a matter of course that he had ended a relationship just a few months earlier with a woman he had been seeing for a few years. I was so totally relieved to hear that tidy tidbit I could barely contain myself. First, if it were true, he was single. Secondly, if it were true, it meant he was decidedly not gay. I told him about my past relationships and how I was not very lucky with men. He learned that I had also ended a relationship about a year earlier as well.

Fausto asked me how long I would be in Rome, and if he could take my mother and me out for dinner the following evening. As if I had any doubt, he naturally said he knew of a great *ristorante* right near our hotel. He said he could come and pick us up after he met his *notaio*, which I surmised was a sort of real estate lawyer as he was closing on a new apartment the very next day. It didn't take very long, but by now I had caught on that Fausto was a typical Italian *mamma's boy*. Here he was, 44 years old, and finally purchasing his own pad. Like many an Italian male, he had lived at home with his *mamma* up until the ripe old age of 35. He looked at me quizzically, innocently pressing the point, *"Why would I want to leave my (h)ome? I get served beautiful pasta, my clothes are always pearrfectly ironed, and I don't pay rent!"* Put that way, it sounded sensible. But, for my American sensibilities, a couple of extra decades sleeping in my childhood bedroom, well…I wouldn't do it for all the plates of pasta in the world. And besides, it'd be me who'd be preparing it and having to do the ironing as well. When he finally left home, he did what any red-blooded Italian would do—he moved in right across the street. I didn't quite know what to make of it. In some respects, it was endearing; but then again, perhaps a little creepy.

I told him we'd be in Rome only for another day. Moreover, I thought we would be able to meet up with him, seeing that we really didn't have any plans for the following evening, our last night in Rome. We got back in the car, and he told me that he wanted to take me to what he considered the most romantic spot in all of Rome, *Monte Mario*. Clearly throwing caution to the wind, I agreed, and we started the long drive up Mount Mario, which in my book could have been Mount Everest; the climb seemed endless. Along the way, Fausto entertained me with more of his amusing stories, told with his delightfully disarming and always candid delivery.

I heard all about his private audience with the Pope: *"You see, my grandfather was Corrado Mezzana, a famous painter in Italy. Have you heard of him?"* Naturally, I had not. I thought to myself, the Mezzana name didn't quite make it into the American household lexicon. Pretty much no one besides Michelangelo did either. Fausto continued: *"He was commissioned by the Vatican for twainty yares to paint some of dee most famous churches. Maybe tomorrow if you have time I would like to take you to see his most famous one—the Sacred Ahrt (Heart) in Santa Maria Sopra Minerva."* He carried on, informing me that the next time I came to Rome he would show me his grandfather's brick. Little did he know it had been 20 years between my last trip and this one. He better not hold his breath. And besides, I had absolutely no idea what he was talking about. I asked if he didn't mean a plaque of some sort. Fausto explained that the Great Door of Pardoning, or Holy Door, leading into St Peter's is bricked up on one side, opened only during the Pope's Jubilee. His grandfather, like many artists over time, received one of the bricks as a special souvenir when the door had been opened last. He had created a small relief atop of it, attesting to his being commissioned as an artist for the Pope. *"Because (h)ee did so much for da Vaticano, we ware given a private meeting with da Pope and I keessed hees ring. I still remember that day even though I was just a baby."* Turns out, he was a 14-year-old baby. It wouldn't take me long to recognize that Fausto used the word 'baby' to indicate his age from the time he was born up until he turned 18 years old.

When we finally reached the top of the hill, he put his hand over my eyes. All in good fun, but I understood then and there that I trusted this curious chap. He drove over to his desired spot then stopped the car right in its tracks. He then told me to open my eyes. Splayed out in front of me was all of Rome, exactly the way the Roman birds view Rome. The dome of St Peter's, all of Vatican City, the Colosseum, the tiny hills of Rome and the sparkling of thousands of even tinier lights on outcrops further afield, monument after monument, majestically laid out in every direction. I had never seen such a stupendous sight. The tops of the buildings, the church domes, the flying saucer roof of the Pantheon; they all looked like you could grab hold of them between two fingers. *"Magnifico!"* I said, and before I had a chance to say anything further, Fausto leaned over and kissed me. He whispered that it was our strange destiny that we met this evening. Later, I would learn that he used this phrase for just about most everything. *"Strange destiny,"* was his customary remark about anything he thought was a coincidence or that took a strange turn of events. Strange or not, I could have cared less. It was all so romantic I thought I might pass out right in his arms from sensory overload. So much for his being gay.

Our Rome-by-Night tour guide

On our way back to the hotel, Fausto suddenly came to a quick stop right in front of an all-night pharmacy on the *Via del Tritone*. Darting out of the car, he said, *"I'll be right back."* I called after him, "Where are you going at this time of night?" He deadpanned, *"I am going to get my drugs."* Great. So that explained the erratic behavior, his fast-paced banter, his parking maneuvers. I started growing a bit nervous but seeing that we weren't far from the hotel, I figured I could always get out and walk back. I couldn't help but think that he didn't seem the type to take drugs, but maybe that was a telltale sign. Or worse, what if he were a drug dealer? I started envisioning the headlines in the papers the next morning: *American girl arrested with Roman drug dealer.* My mom would be devastated; she had placed so much trust in this perfectly Roman perfect stranger. When he got back to the car, I heaved a sigh of relief. He had pulled out of his pharmacy bag a package of breath mints called *Frisk.* I suppose it could have been worse; they could have been a pack of condoms called *Frisky.*

I arrived back at the hotel to find my mother sitting up in bed, clearly anxious over my whereabouts. Fausto and I had been gone for hours and she didn't even know his full name. I reassured her that all was okay (careful to omit the part in which for a moment I thought he might be into drugs). Her inner voice had been right all along; Fausto was a very nice guy, courteous to a fault, and all in all, it turned out to be a sensational, serendipitous evening. Too tired to talk, and too many emotions running through my mind, I told her I would fill her in on the details the next morning over breakfast.

As I got ready for bed, I thought to myself that something had, indeed, happened to me that night. I lay in bed thinking about the very strangeness of destiny: the fountain, Fausto, my mother coming on this trip instead of some loser, the coins…until I realized it was 3 am and I seriously needed to get some sleep.

CHAPTER IV

❧

The Lion King

Butterflies were busy flittering away in my stomach when I woke up the next morning. I could do nothing but go over and over again each moment of the night before in my head. At breakfast, when my mom finally came to the end of her banter, all I could make out was, "So—do you think it's a good plan for today?" I snapped out of my dreamy thoughts realizing I had not heard a word she had uttered. "So—what *really* happened last night?" she asked inquisitively. "This Fausto must have really shown you a pretty great time." She tried to act coy, but I knew she was bursting at the seams. "Well, actually, yes, mom—it was one of the best evenings I have had in a long time…Oh and I am so sorry I wasn't paying attention to what you were saying." Seeing the twinkle in my eye, in response, she simply shook her head, asking, "Can you at least tell me at what point you stopped listening to me so I don't have to repeat *everything* I've said?!"

We wanted to make the most of our last full day in Rome, so off we went by subway over to St Peter's Basilica and the Vatican Museums. Saint Peter's is quite an eyeful to behold with its hundreds of artworks, statues, objects, drapes and chapels crowding the entire church from floor to ceiling. Surrounded by so many Madonnas in paint, plaster, marble and gold leaf was mind-boggling. My mother's most prized possession had been her statue of the Madonna. For years, all I can remember is her shouting out from one room or another to us kids, "No throwing the ball in the house! You'll ruin my Madonna!" Inevitably, my brother Tony caught an amazing pass. But in the process, he bumped into her statue as if it was a linebacker, smashing her Madonna to smithereens. Years later, he would redeem himself by replacing it with an exact replica he had found on ebay.

Michelangelo's *Pietà*, a mother cradling her dead son as if he was just a tiny baby nearly brought us both to tears. Turning down the long transept, we were then both stopped right in our tracks. We stood there frozen with astonishment at the sight of the enormous canopy set atop four massive, twisting bronze columns right in the middle of the Basilica. The ray of golden light beaming down from the dome or *cupola* shined like a spotlight on this incredible work of art, created at the gifted hands of Gian Lorenzo Bernini. Dwarfed by its magnificence, we overheard a tour guide saying that the four columns were 20 meters high. My mom, ever the ready math teacher, quickly calculated it to be about 65 feet tall. We overheard the guide explain the source of the bronze that Bernini used to make the structure: "You see, this has been a contemporary controversy, although it is commonly believed to have been taken from the roof or *portico* ceiling of the Pantheon." Naturally, I couldn't resist the temptation to walk over to her and say that I had heard the bronze had come from the Colosseum. "Well, there are many theories of where the bronze came from, but the Pantheon is believed to be the most accurate." I made a note to myself to make sure to tell Fausto to update his *Rome-by-Night* tour with this fact so the next American girl he picks up would, in the very least, not be led astray, culturally speaking.

Later that afternoon, I left my mom back at the hotel so she could take a nap. My poor mom. She had spent most of her adult life in a futile bid to get a moment of shuteye. Working and running our wild household by day, while catering to a husband who worked nights, she would take any lull in the high jinx to try and sneak away. "Even if the house is burning down...*Don't wake me up!*" she would admonish us. I think it was only after we all left home that she ever did get a good night's sleep; but even then, with children flung across the country, she'd be up at all hours of the night worrying about someone or another or coaching one of us by phone across the miles. I decided to take the opportunity to go for a long run in Rome's Central Park—the *Villa Borghese*, once the hunting grounds for popes and cardinals and Roman elite. The entire time, I could think about nothing but the events of the night before, replaying them like a favorite album in my head. How extemporaneous it had all been and what hand "strange destiny" indeed had played in crossing Fausto's and my paths. Of all the people buzzing about all of Rome, I couldn't believe my luck at having met someone so highly entertaining. Of course, the bonus was having met someone whom I also found so totally attractive. Was I falling for someone who lived a continent away? Me, a flighty California girl, he a proud Roman? Did it really matter? Once again, I reminded myself of my own turn at destiny: *Lucky at work, Unlucky at love...* I tried in vain to put my thoughts aside, one way or the other. Besides, after tonight, I may never see nor hear from him again. Nevertheless, I still couldn't help but wonder what the fates had in store for the coming attraction. It was our last night in Rome, and Fausto would be picking us up around 7 o'clock for an Italian evening out on the town.

The phone rang in our hotel room around 5:30 pm. It was Fausto calling to firm up our dinner plans. *"Hello,"* he said, *"I am Fausto, remember me, from last night?"* Of course—how in the world could I forget him? I had thought of nothing else all day long. *"I want to confirm dee time to peek you and your mother up dis evening."* I told him that anytime around 7 o'clock would be fine. There was a momentary silence. Which turned out to be the quiet before the storm. Thus followed an onslaught of questions: *"Are you sure you want to eat so airly? How can you eat so soon after your lunch? Why do all Americans eat so airly?*" Clearly baffled by my request, he pressed on…"*You know, in Roma, no one eats before 9 pm.*" I replied that while I was certain that there was a great deal of truth to that statement, it was difficult to change a lifetime of eating habits in just two weeks. This was one instance in which I most likely could not persuade my Irish-American mother to act like a Roman. Before we could reach an agreement on a more acceptable dinnertime, Fausto, in his stream of consciousness parlance, began telling me about his day. He told me he had just left the office of his *notaio* and had finally closed on the purchase of the apartment he had been living in for the past ten years. "*You know, Caterina, another strange destiny (h)appened today…One (h)our before I signed dee final documents, the owner of the apartment died! His niece phoned my notaio to say that she wanted to stop the sale. Lucky for me, I had transferred the money into the owner's bank account <u>yesterday</u>—and he signed the papers a day before…Do you understand what a strange destiny it was meeting you last night? And then, this (h)appening? I teenk you are breenging me good luck!*" His unbridled enthusiasm was certainly contagious.

When Fausto showed up at the hotel at our renegotiated time of 7:30 pm, my mother called down to him from her open window on the *Via Veneto*. It was a classic scene reminiscent of an old, Italian movie. I was flabbergasted to hear her say that she was tired and wanted to stay in for the night. She suggested that the two of us go out together for a nice evening meal. Staring at my mom in disbelief, I told her that I really wanted her to join us. Giving me one of her *Mama knows best* looks, she insisted, "No, honey, you go alone. It's your last night on this terrific trip, and I think it's important that you two spend it together." I thanked her effusively and bolted downstairs, taking two at a time, sanguine at the prospect of being—*alone*—with this captivating Italian man. I hopped in the car and braced myself for another white-knuckle adventure with Fausto careening around the tiny, trafficked streets of Rome.

He told me he wanted to take me to a typical *spaghetteria* located on a small alleyway near the *Trevi Fountain*. We could take a stroll after dinner, except this time, he forbade me to throw in any more coins. He said he picked the restaurant because you could choose amongst 50 types of spaghetti dishes; since he knew that most Americans were never very easy to please, they were bound to have something that I would like. We were seated at an outdoor table positioned practically on the cobblestone alley. Throughout dinner we were entertained by a stream of *Vespa* motor scooters and cars racing by just inches from our table. We chatted all evening long, but all I can remember is thinking to myself how much I enjoyed being in this place with this man, hearing his hysterical stories. When I told him I had taken a long run in the beautiful park of *Villa Borghese* and was surprised to find a zoo right in the middle of it, Fausto segued into one of his hilarious antidotes: *"You know, when I was a baby, my mamma took me to see the lions in da zoo there—and I was a very curious boy, you know. When the lion came close to us, I put my finger right in the ass of the lion!"* I burst out laughing while Fausto continued, unflinchingly: *"Mia mamma—who was wearing a long necklace of white pearls—pulled my finger out and pulled me away with her as we rolled down the cement path away from the lion house. But in her (h)urry, I grabbed onto hair necklace,"* he said gesticulating madly. *"We stayed until darrk tryeeng to collect all the small pairls dat broke away, but eet was impossible to find dem all. She didn't let me eat dolce* (dessert) *for over two mont(h)s after dat."*

Imagining the entire sequence of events unfolding kept me in stitches. Fausto seemed to have an insatiable curiosity for almost everything. Even as a baby in a stroller, he didn't seem afraid of anyone or anything, not even a lion. He followed up his tale with what I would come to recognize as one of his usual *non sequiturs*. Playfully, he asked, *"But can you tell me (h)ow you can go back to America after eating our Italian food for two weeks?"* I replied that in actual fact I loved to cook and didn't dine out regularly in restaurants. So the entire experience here had been a real treat. He told me that he had been to America several times and that his favorite restaurant was one called *Denny's*. Not for the first time that evening, my eyes widened into huge orbs. I thought to myself, "You have *got* to be kidding." I prayed that if I was still in contact with this man after this evening, that he would never *ever* tell anyone I know on Earth that this was his favorite American eating establishment. *"Do you know dees restaurant my love? Eet's fantasteek dees restaurant, and we don't have anything like teese in Italy. You know, you can eat all you want for just four point 99?"* It took a moment, but I finally deciphered that he meant to say 4 dollars and 99 cents, but before I could correct him, I just started to giggle.

The conversation turned to how we could see each other again. I told him that I thought he was such a sweet guy, but I lived half a planet away, and frankly, he was sort of geographically undesirable. He offered that maybe he could finagle something with Alitalia in order to get me a ticket to come back to Rome. Like his drug purchase the night before, I had absolutely no idea what 'doing something' signified in Fausto terms. For all I knew he was dating one of the girls at the ticket counter. But I quickly cast those thoughts aside while we had fun entertaining the idea of carrying on a cross-country relationship. As we got up from the table to leave, Fausto leaned over and kissed me passionately. He held my face in his beautiful hands and told me that we absolutely had to find a way to see each other again. He asked me once again if I believed in destiny, adding for good measure, that it was fate that had caused us to meet at the fountain.

Hand in hand, we headed over to *our* fountain. I couldn't wait to thank it for bringing the two of us together. It seemed more luminous and even more dazzling than the night before. Perhaps it was because the moon was more full, or perhaps it was fate twinkling her eyes at the sight of the two of us there. Whatever it was, I knew that I had never felt so incredibly happy with someone in my entire life. Fausto, feeling the same way, invited me back over to his apartment for a nightcap. I could hear my mom telling me to live each day like it was my last. So instead of tossing coins, I threw the die, thinking "What the heck?!" I was going to seize this moment and relish every single second until I had to go back to my loveless, lackluster life.

Back at his miniscule apartment, Fausto poured out some *sambuca* before sitting down to serenade me at the piano for hours. It reminded me of nights growing up with my dad rehearsing or holding jam sessions with his group. He would be on piano, his band members belting out Sinatra or Bacharach on trumpet, guitar, bass, drums and sax. Watching Fausto at the keys, I could see his undeniable passion for music. In reality, Fausto seemed to throw himself into most everything he did. When he got up off the piano bench, we fell straight into each other's arms.

I woke up with a start a few hours later, awash with the knowledge that I needed to get back to my hotel, pack my bags and catch a plane back to California. I was panic-stricken. What time was it? What about my mom? Would she be waiting up for me this entire time? Although it was difficult to leave his embrace, I knew I had to hightail it out of there—and fast. But before heading back to the hotel, Fausto pulled another of his *Rome-by-Night* surprises. He insisted we stop at his favorite *pasticceria*, a little all-night bakery near *Porta Pia* that opens at midnight to bake the next day's bread. There, one could buy fresh-baked chocolate-filled croissants and Danish pastries with hot white and dark chocolate poured over top. It was pure bliss. Always the gallant man, he picked up a few extra, and handing them to me said, *"You must take some back for your mamma for her breakfast."* Arriving at my hotel, we said our goodbyes and goodnights...with Fausto's departing words, *"Buona notte, amore...Goodnight, my love..."*

I sneaked up the rickety wooden stairs as silently as I could. By this time, it *was* 4 am. Slowly opening the door to crawl quietly into bed, I was surprised to find my mother sitting up in bed, reading. "Mom! What are you doing up?!" She said she simply couldn't sleep, growing by this time quite nervous that I had gone off until all hours of the night with a total stranger. "I realized I hadn't even taken Fausto's phone number in case something had happened." So, I guess she didn't always practice what she preached about *carpe diem*. But now it was my turn not to get any sleep. I decided to take a quick bath and then pack my suitcase. Mary Lee reached inside the bag that I had left on her bedside table with Fausto's still-warm chocolate croissants inside. She called from the bedroom that the croissant was heavenly...and asked why we hadn't thought to buy a few more for our long trip home. My mother would rather have chocolate or nuts than any other food substance. Then and there, I knew that Fausto had won my mom right over. An hour later, our taxi pulled up to carry us out of romantic Rome and drop us at the airport. It would be 14 hours before we would land in chaotic Los Angeles, an entire world away.

CHAPTER V

Moonstruck

reat. Fourteen hours to mull over the reruns and coming attractions of my very own scheduled series, *"Unlucky in love, Lucky at work,"* starring yours, truly. Here I was, 39 years old, and I had finally met a decent man I really liked; someone who made me laugh and someone with whom I really thought I could stay forever— and he lived halfway 'round the world. Talk about 'strange destiny.' It felt more like a stricken destiny to me. I spent the entire plane ride going back through every frame of these last two extraordinary days over and over again in my head; rewind—play-back—rewind. In the very least, I could dream about this gift of a guy who the fates had set me up with on a blind date. It would still offer a dash of color to my perfectly uneventful life. Looking over at me by her side, my mom asked, "Honey—are you okay? You look so sad." I told her that I was just tired out. But in reality, I was already feeling those odd pangs of longing for this ornery Roman I had met only two days before.

Back home in San Diego, I was greeted by my two stupendous Siamese cats, Thelma & Louise. They were overjoyed to see me, and I was thrilled to see them. Surveying my empty home, I was even more ecstatic at not finding my ex-husband still milling about the house. Without a loafer of an ex to deal with, the house was positively tranquil. For the first time in nearly the entire span of my existence, I was *Home Alone*. I looked around me. No siblings, no roommates, no live-in boyfriends, no husbands. It felt quite peculiar. At face value, I had everything. But in reality, I felt I had nothing. I was overcome with insecurities about what the future would bring; that is, if it brought anything at all.

What if this romantic interlude with a dapper Italian was nothing but a short-lived commercial break in my soap opera of a life? What if he actually had a steady girlfriend? Or worse, a wife? What if I was falling for yet another non-committal guy? What if I were just fooling myself that this was the real deal? After all, he may be a smooth salesman and I, a desperate buyer. Some guys have a keen radar trained to pick up on women like me; and they're the same guys who take countless women straight to the cleaners. Women's magazines are full of relationship horror stories, but I didn't need to read about it—I had lived through the entire table of contents of that book time and time again. My choice picks ran the gamut from the son of a Chicago mafia Don (who fortunately let me off the hook lightly) to a guy with a drinking problem, to the most recent one, a penniless pathological liar who tried to bury me in a mountain of debt. No surprise that taken together, all of the men formed a composite sketch of my father. Looking at Fausto in this light, it wasn't a pretty sight. I was fairly confident that Fausto was a hardworking guy who didn't hit the bottle (aside from the occasional glass of *limoncello*), and as far as I could tell, one who didn't make light of the truth, either. Then again, he was good looking like my dad, he played the piano like my dad, and, I couldn't get around this clincher; he was indeed a red-blooded Italian, just like dear ol' dad. I couldn't decide whether to file these in the 'plus' column or the 'negative' side in the balance sheet of my brain. Truth be told, in our 16-hour whirlwind romance, this somewhat unconventional guy

40

came off to me as someone I could actually count on. Fausto seemed thoughtful, loyal, and totally respectful of what it took to earn a buck, and save it. Certainly, if this fledgling relationship went further than a nightcap at his pad I would have already come a long way since my ex bought a cruise *As seen on TV* using his ex-wife's credit cards. Or the time he had signed all the papers at a timeshare presentation the instant I had gotten up to go to the bathroom. I always seemed to jump into it with both feet, but unlike my cats, I never landed truly on my feet. Would this be another in my litany of relationship wreckages?

What would this bizarre burgeoning romance lead to? Probably nothing. Jet-lagged and restless, I got up in the middle of the night to check my inbox. As if purposely penned to stem the swelling of waves of unfounded fears, I was both astounded and elated to find ten emails from Fausto. Relieved that my ex-husband wasn't around to snoop into my inbox and listen to my messages as he had done in the past, I figured that this might be a sign that Fausto didn't have a prying wife either. Or in the very least, he didn't have one prying into his outbox. I read each of his missives, relishing in the delight of his outlandish barbs:

"My love—living without you is like eating my macaroni without the parmigiano cheese"

"When I kissed you it was like when the flame touches the petrol and there is an explosion in the night"

"I can't wait to see you again so I can squeeze you like a lemon"

"Waking up by myself is like eating my pizza without my anchovies"

I would quickly discover that for Italians, everything involves either food or animals, or both. I was absolutely tickled pink and quite relieved. So I hadn't been the only one playing reruns of the last 48 hours. I jotted a brief note back to Fausto before falling fast asleep, calmed by the thought that he, too, had been thinking about me. Perhaps our chance encounter hadn't been simply a flight of fancy. Perhaps it was perfectly fitting to fly high thinking of him while we were apart. Until crash landing the next evening, that is.

I went out with my usual gaggle of girlfriends, absolutely percolating with the news of all that had transpired in Rome. I might as well have told them I had caught tuberculosis. Unanimously, and in their best *"been there, done that"* wisdom, they weighed in on my Italian stallion. The verdict? He was probably a dyed-in-the-wool "fountain hanger." His country's *Latin Lover* reputation had unfortunately preceded him—by sheer volumes. They warned me that I should be very careful of Italian men, and that I, of all people, on the rebound and what with my father running out on his wife and kids, should be more wary than anyone. Unsure what their evidence was based on, they concluded their narrative with the entirely true legend that most gallant Italian men had a wife, a lover, and a couple of kids tucked away for good measure. I countered, to a set of raised eyebrows, that actually, Fausto told me he had never been married. As a matter-of-fact, Fausto had told me that in his 45 years he had never found a woman he had loved enough to marry. I might as well have been preaching in Chinese to a room of deaf mutes. In our Golden Age of sarcasm, surely not a one of my friends bought into this old yarn. They chalked the whole romantic interlude up to *An Affair to Remember*, telling me to fondle the memory, but to just forget the guy. Those two romantic evenings with Fausto should be just a nice recollection to take home from Rome, like a cheap souvenir.

Needless to say, I returned home totally depressed. They were probably right. I should just forget about that 'fountain hanger' Fausto and move on with my new life. I turned on my answering machine to listen to my messages. All from Fausto. *"Hello, I am Fausto, wair are you my love? Are you t(h)rowing coins into the fountains of San Diego? Please phone me when you are home...Mi manchi...I miss you..."* Just hearing his voice again put a smile back on my face. I thought to myself, "My girlfriends don't know what he's like...and besides, even if he *is* a 'fountain hanger,' he was the sweetest one I'd ever met." In the end, I had given myself a lift, picked myself up like *tiramisu*. I decided to ignore the naysayers and not let them put a dent in my shiny new romance. Steadfast now in my resolve, I determined to do whatever I could to see Fausto again. And besides, I couldn't wait to get a slew of silly messages from him. I looked at my kitchen clock; with a nine-hour difference, it was too late to phone him. I would send him an email and wait for his call the next morning. Happily, I took a bath and jumped in bed with Thelma & Louise dreaming of fountains, lions and pizza with anchovies.

Feeling much more high-spirited, the next day I went for my morning run on the beach. Back at home, I was surprised that I hadn't heard from my zany Romeo. Although I was a bit disappointed, I figured he was just busy at work. But then, another day passed and I still hadn't heard from him. Then another. Nor the day after that. Four days with no word from Fausto; no adoring messages, no charming emails, *silenzio*... My heart sunk. Once again, in a long line of charming, sweet-talking men, I had managed to convince myself that this one might have been different; that I had found someone who would be on my side for once, rooting for me in my corner, and not withholding their love and attention. I had called straight up from central casting my type yet again. My friends had been right all along. By now, Fausto had probably already fished another American girl out of the fountain, and was telling her that she was the Parmesan cheese on his eggplant *parmigiano*.

I felt like such a fool. How could I have thought that this could have gone somewhere? I started reenacting the push-me/pull-you of burgeoning relationships: *Just get on with your life...But what if he's a really great guy? Try and find somebody real, somebody American, someone who lived in your own zip code...But he's so charming and nice...Someone who wasn't just like your dad...* I felt the very same way I had felt the day my dad left and never came back home: sheer emptiness, uncertainty about my future, betrayal. After a wave of loneliness would wash over me, I'd summon up a new source of fortitude. Besides, I'd been down this path plenty of times before, and I was totally good for the wear. I would pine away for my dad, but was met with silence in return. To outsiders, he was always playing 'Man of the House' when that's exactly what he had been doing—playing all of us so he could play in his band, play with his gals, and then cash in his chips without so much as a goodbye.

Hoping beyond hope that maybe this time it'd be different, I made a last ditch attempt to win Fausto back. Like those tiny flares they send up in the air before releasing the missile, I sent a few more missives to him at work. I wanted so much to hear that it was all a mistake. He hadn't simply dismissed me. No reply. Maybe his wife *could* crack his email box. More messages, stone silence. I scanned the entire audience anxiously, row by row, seat by seat, to see if I could spot my dad seated comfortably at Orchestra Hall. First, the orchestra; then left side, then right. Eyeballing the balcony seats, row by row, all the way up to the rafters. No sign of him. I was sure he loved us as much as his new kids. But he wasn't there. Afterwards, I kept casing the foyer in the off chance that I had missed him. Finally, I had to admit to myself that he never even bothered to show up. It was now one full week since Fausto's last phone message. Just like guys who never return calls, and are too chicken to call it quits. At least he owed me an email explanation. Nowadays, you didn't even have to speak to break it off with someone. Girlfriends are always right. Just like all the other times before, I knew I'd get over this disappointment as well. Disheartened and lovesick and not in the right way, I decided to send him one last brief message: *Did you go to the moon, my love?*

By the time the weekend came around, I was thoroughly miserable. I spent my every waking moment tossing around in my head like a *Cirque du Soleil* juggler all of the variables as to what might have brought on the sea change that had first swept me up into that tidal wave of heart-racing romance. In an attempt to look on the bright side, I'd try and convince myself that at least it had been fun while it lasted. Settling into my desk at work that following Monday morning, I was crestfallen. I had picked the wrong kind of guy. One more time. How long would I carry the curse of a fly-by-night father into my relationships? Opening my inbox, I was completely bowled over. There they were, ten emails from Fausto, my footloose and fancy free Roman fountain hanger.

"*Oh, my love, Perdonami! (Forgive me)—I am back from the moon!*"

Although it put a smile on my face, I thought to myself, "Yeah. Right. What does that mean?" He probably had gotten in a fight with a wife or girlfriend who had found him out and she cancelled his email account. I read on, practically rolling my eyes in the process:

"Someone had tried to kill me!! I was poisoned!"

Sure. His girlfriend, after she had found all his emails to me.

"My love, you can't believe what happened. I was <u>dying</u>... And was on my deathbed at home—without being able to feed myself. I ate one dish of cozze (mussels) *that were not clean—and I was poisoned!!!"*

By far, this would go down as tops in the annals of totally outrageous excuses.

"Do you know what I am saying...? They are trying to kill me in my own town?!"

I started to giggle. He was so dramatic. I mean, *who* on Earth would be trying to kill him...I mean, who did he think he was...Caesar?

"It was a strange destiny, my love...I was going there for many years and never did this happen to me...Now, I discover they are closing the restaurant...Strange destiny, don't you agree? My mamma had to come over to give me food because I was so weak and completely destroyed."

Phew. I thanked God it was his mother who came to his rescue. Although it was a most outlandish story, coming from Fausto for some reason, my faith had been restored in believing in strange destiny. Even if it did give you food poisoning.

"When will we see each other again? I need to see you...When can you come back to Roma?"

Runaway Vacation

I wrote back to him that I had to fly shortly to New York for an investment conference. Perhaps I could take a plane from there to come and see him. The only catch was that unfortunately, I had already used up all my vacation days and I didn't think my boss would let me take any more time off. The reaction was immediate. "*Whatdaaa?!!?*" Whenever he was surprised at something, out would come the "*Whatdaa?!*" in astonished reply, as in, 'What the heck?!' *You don't have more than two weeks a year?! Are the companies in America completely crazy? Can't you speak to your boss and see if he will let you come for five days? I can send you the teecket from New York if you want...We can speak about how we can work this out when you get here...About making you my partner and you can have my teeckets... Okay, my love??*"

Before I had time to think it through, the very next day I received a confirmation email for a ticket from New York to Rome compliments from Fausto. I was really going back to Rome! I immediately phoned my mom and asked if she was sitting down. "Yes, what happened honey, Adam didn't come back did he?" "No," I replied, but Fausto had. And not only that, I was on my way back to see him and our resplendently romantic Rome. In just a few weeks' time. Fausto may have been back from the moon, but I was totally over it. He made me feel so wanted, so loved, and so needed...At first my mom was shocked at the news. But true to form, she then told me to "*Go for it!*" She had always encouraged each of us to take risks and never back down on pursuing whatever it was we wanted out of life. With the whirlwind of emotions and activity surrounding my idiosyncratic Italian, I couldn't help but think what more would a girl want out of life. With Fausto, I would certainly never be bored. I knew I had to go.

Sitting at my desk, ticket practically in hand, I mustered up the courage and decided to meet strange destiny head-on. I phoned my boss and simply explained the situation: That I really needed to take this chance, that I had finally met someone that I thought could be the man of my life, and that if I didn't do this, I would regret it for the rest of my days...I told him that I understood if he said no, but that I was going to go anyway...I don't know if it was just to get me off the phone or if inside, he was a romantic, but he finally gave his consensus, but only for three days. He said that if I wasn't back by the following Wednesday he would have to find somebody else to replace me. Sales were sales and money was money. I was so ecstatic that I didn't even know when Wednesday was. I felt like Cinderella getting to go to the ball.

Packing my bags for the conference, I had to work out what to bring. Not only did I need business attire, but I also had to think about what I would wear in Rome when re-meeting my handsome prince. I wanted to look more like Monica Bellucci than Katie Couric. I raced to the airport and hopped on my flight, gripping my Italian dictionary like a child holding onto her dolly. I landed in New York on Sunday afternoon; the opening reception would take place that evening at the Grand Hyatt Hotel.

The three-day conference was a total blur. All I could do to get through the droning of speeches, the dinners, the coffee breaks, was count down 'til takeoff. I looked at my watch incessantly: six hours, then four hours, then two hours, I would be off to Rome again. Twenty years had gone by between my first and second trip to Rome, but this time it was a matter of weeks. I couldn't help but think how crazy this whole thing was. I hardly knew this man, and here I was, flying across the ocean to be back in his arms after having practically just met over dinner and a drive (or rather, a drive and then dinner). The things we do for love. Or, if it were not quite unbridled love, at least it would be five passionate days with an incredibly sexy man.

Practically running from the conference, I grabbed a taxi for JFK. But once at the airport I went to check-in and had the shock of my life. For some inexplicable reason I could not for the life of me find my ticket. Panicking, I started emptying out my purse, rifling through my briefcase, nothing. Where in the world could it have gone? I nervously started to retrace all my steps in my mind. Could I have left it in my hotel room? In the taxi? Was this some bizarre trick of fate? Was it one of my mom's GMCs—God-Manufactured Coincidence messages telling me I shouldn't be going to Italy after all? I explained my predicament to the counter staff, telling them that I had a special ticket sent to me from an Alitalia employee. I begged them to check their records. I paced nervously while waiting to see if they would let me on the plane. I watched the time go by. Nothing. I checked my bags again. I pleaded my case.

I stood there nearly in tears as the last person in line handed over her passport. After all was said and done, I would not be living out my particular Italian fantasy. I was crestfallen.

But as luck would have it, or, as they used to say in ancient Rome…'I guess destiny smiled upon me this very day.' Just as they were getting ready to close the flight, the Alitalia manager said he had finally found my record. He added that I would have to run to the gate in order to make the flight. I ran as fast as my legs could carry me, boarded the plane, and slumped, worn out from the conference and this ninth inning stretch, right into my seat. In flight, I tried to get some shut-eye, but awoke with a start as I began second-guessing the whole affair. I recalled the old movie, *Coffee Tea or Me?* In fact, I told myself, this stuff only happens in the movies. But at 30,000 feet there was certainly no turning back now.

The next thing I heard was the pilot's announcement to prepare for landing. We would be arriving at Rome's *Fiumicino Airport* in just 20 minutes and that the weather—this hot summer's day—was sunny and clear. I waited for my bag, went through customs and egressed through the large sliding glass doors. No sign of Fausto. When we landed, it was actually *the day after* from when we had departed and I wondered if Fausto had somehow mixed up the dates. Families, couples, car service drivers holding signs; it seemed that everyone was being met by someone—everyone, that is, except me. Slowly, with equal parts apprehension and expectation, I ventured outside the Arrivals Terminal. Still no sight of Fausto. A rather large pit started to grow in my stomach. Heaving a heavy sigh, I imagined he had played me for a fool. What a mistake to come all this way for a man you hardly even knew. Begrudgingly, I went over to ask the Alitalia ticket agent when the next flight back to New York was, just in case he never showed up. "Tomorrow morning at 10:05 but the flight is already full." "Great," I thought. "Just fantastic luck on my side once again." Or, was Lady Luck doing me a favor by showing me that I had bet on the wrong horse?

My heart sinking practically into the pavement, I started pacing up and down, past the taxi stand, surveying all of the cars parked— looking out for Fausto's black Audi 80; the same sleek car that he had taken me and my mom in on our wacky *Rome-by-Night* tour. How they all looked alike during the day! I searched my purse for his address. Perhaps there had been some misunderstanding, or he had simply gotten tied up in traffic. Perhaps I could just take a taxi over to his house and wait for him to come home. Then again, what if I showed up and his wife answers the door? Perhaps I should take a cab over there just for that very reason. Feeling more dejected by the moment, suddenly, I felt two warm hands cover my eyes... *"Bentornata" a Roma!—Welcome back to Rome!"* I heard a familiar voice say. I turned around to see Fausto—even more handsome than I had remembered him. He was wearing a beautiful suit and very Italian sunglasses that made him look like a mixture between Marcello Mastroianni and Harrison Ford. *"Bentornata,* indeed," I thought. He was Italian, and timeliness is decidedly not their forte. But seeing him again, all my fears were vanquished in an instant by his big, broad smile. I had to admit that, yes, indeed, it was nice to be back.

He kissed me, grabbed my bag and then whisked me into his car all the while asking me if I was angry. Thinking that he meant by his tardiness, I tried to play it cool. "Angry? Angry about what?" Or, perhaps he meant the week that he dropped all communications supposedly lying in bed with food poisoning, hovering between life and death. *"No..."* he repeated, *"Are you angry? I mean, do you want to eat someteeng?!"* It finally dawned on me that he meant hungry with an 'h'—a sound that Italians cannot bring themselves to pronounce, try as they might. For Fausto, 'hotel' would be delivered with the shock of 'Oh!-tel', 'home' groaned with 'oam.' I would have to get used to his quirky accent once again. I was looking forward to it.

Twenty minutes later, we were being seated at a small outdoor restaurant in Rome's *Campo dei Fiori*; a lovely medieval *piazza* filled with *bancarelle*—market stalls selling everything from fish to flowers, and people bustling about at all hours of the day or night. Fausto made a point of saying that he liked this particular place, but not for its character; because here, the food was always good and their *cozze* (mussels) were not going to kill you. Again and again, I was amused over how dramatic he could be about every little thing, right down to the tiny pink mussels buried in your plate of pasta.

After our delicious lunch eating non-assassin mussels, Fausto suggested I go and take a nap. So as not to come off too easy, or, as we say in sales, to not appear as 'a desperate salesman' or in my case, 'a desperate buyer,' I had decided that it would be prudent to reserve a hotel room. I booked a room overlooking all of Rome, at the prestigious *Cavalieri Hilton Hotel*. It offered the same beautiful view I had seen that very night my love life turned the page, and just going up that hill thrilled me right down to the tips of my toes. Needless to say, it was a precautionary measure but quite a marvelous one at that; a luxurious last resort just in case Fausto didn't turn out to be the sweet, lovely, funny Italian man I thought he was. Besides, if it turned out my girlfriends were right all along, at least I'd have a few days by a glorious pool looking out over all Rome to work on my tan and drown my sorrows in glass upon glass of *prosecco*.

Fausto, accompanying me up to my room, said that he would come by later and pick me up for dinner. Tucking me in, he kissed me softly, saying he would be back around 8:30. As I drifted off to sleep, I felt as though I had just landed in Never Neverland; a place without any worries or cares, a place where I'd wake up to a handsome prince and a passionate kiss. Working in the hotel business, I thought it poetic justice that I had become accustomed to sleeping in luxury hotels. It made up for the umpteen years sleeping four to a room with my sisters. And even then, we decidedly had it better than the boys. My youngest brother, Reno, was called 'The Floater.' He would be thrown on a floor, couch or a bed whenever and wherever he literally dropped off to sleep. When things got tight, my brother Tony took to sleeping outside, having taken up residence inside my dad's organ trailer. That was put to an end when my dad assumed he had run away from home. Seeing him "return" back home, my dad decided to teach him a lesson for having run away in the first place. A friend of mine called the house to tell me that she had just seen my brother tearing past her front door; my dad in hot pursuit—brandishing a gun.

I woke up a few hours later and took a long, hot bath in the gorgeous white marble bathroom. It turned out that I knew the general manager and he had upgraded me to a luxurious suite. Strolling down to the lobby right at 8:30, I was surprised to find my Italian knight—right on time. Donning his standard-issue pair of cool sunglasses (despite being indoors and late in the evening), he greeted me at the base of the monumental red-carpeted staircase. I felt like a movie star. "*Andiamo,*" he said, with a look of sheer, suave confidence. "*Let's go—I made resairrvayyshuns at a nice ristorante close to my ouse that is soopposed to be fantasteek.*"

June in Rome meant it was also already unbearably hot and humid. Most of the Romans had already left for their summer holidays; many choosing the spectacular settings of the islands that Italy has to offer: *Ischia, Ponza, Capri, Sicily, Sardinia.* Although I didn't know it at the time, years later, I can attest that Rome in summertime is actually my favorite place to be. You can always find a parking spot anywhere, even right in the city center, and by 10:00 at night you have the streets to yourself while savoring the most delectable *gelato* to be found anywhere on the planet. The bonus is that most tourists eat at around 7 pm, heading to bed around 10 or 11 pm, so you don't even need reservations at most restaurants. Summer nights in Rome, with its deep purple firmament over red rooftops and dark umbrella pines seems to sparkle with magic. At night, the city turns into an ancient Oz, albeit a Pompeian red, graffiti-laden version of it. It may not have horses of different colors or yellow bricks, but its tiny stone squares charmingly called *Sanpietrini* (after *San Pietro*, Saint Peter) indicating your pathway round yet another fountain or square is the next best thing. As we left for the restaurant, it felt like the city was ours alone; just the two of us under the spell of her enchantment. I couldn't believe I was walking down those cobblestones arm in arm with Fausto. Nothing else mattered to me in the whole, entire world than being right where I was, right with remarkably romantic and fantastically funny Fausto.

Fausto took me to an off-the-beaten-track part of Rome called *San Lorenzo*. It is a sort of rundown area near the *Termini* railway station, a place where you'll find true Romans who have lived there for centuries. When they die, just up the road is the main cemetery Verano housing all the generations who went before. *San Lorenzo* was the only area that was bombed by the Allies during WWII, despite the fact that Rome had been declared an 'Open City.' Thousands perished. So, the architecture is a hodgepodge of pre- and post-war buildings, mixed in with old markets, university buildings and laundry hanging out nearly every window. Bustling with students, it's filled with tiny clubs and eateries of every kind. We went into a small *trattoria* crammed with clients crowded around tight wooden tables, called *Tram Tram*. It was a play on words with the Italian expression, '*tran tran*' meaning the hustle and bustle of life's ins and outs; a perfect metaphor for my busy life back home in the real world. Instead, this little gem of a place, decorated with pieces of 1950s trams was absolute perfection. The *Signora* who ran the place with her chef sister made sure each and every customer had a meal to remember.

I ordered a pasta dish brimming with sardines and *broccoletti*, a Roman type of broccoli that Americans would probably call spinach. It was gorgeously savory and the mix of flavors so interesting that I quickly devoured the entire dish. Given the restaurant's location close to the cemetery I thought I died and went to heaven. Tram Tram was definitely a foodie's paradise. Even if it hadn't been, I probably wouldn't have cared nor would I have noticed. Taking one look at my fish dish, Fausto regaled me once again with his brush with death-by-mussels. He told me he had been so ill that his zealous mamma had to drop everything to come hold vigil by his bedside:

> "You know, she ees completely crazy about the termo meter and she put eet in every hole in my body."

> "I had the termo meter stuck in my ears, my mouth, under my arms and in my culo—ass. I am just now recovering from all the holes she made in me."

Almost as an aside, he added that I'd soon meet *La Mamma*. Thoughts of this overprotective species and their reaction to meeting the person who one day might be responsible for cutting the umbilical tie left me speechless. So I just smiled, thinking

52

it would be best to just let some things pass without comment. Fausto picked up his free association parlance from there. With Fausto, things like even silences were never uncomfortable. I never felt for one moment that I had to work at making conversation with him. In fact, reflecting upon my Willie Loman lifestyle, it was such a joy sharing a table with someone from the opposite sex who I wasn't trying to convince to buy advertising space from me! *Che bello!* How absolutely enchanting was this evening and even more adorable man. So this is what falling in love must feel like.

After a marathon make-out session in the car, we decided to take advantage of my VIP status and enjoy a nightcap in the Executive Lounge at the *Cavalieri Hilton.* Situated on the seventh floor, with plate glass windows offering vistas down to the Eternal City, it has a living room feel decked out with huge sofas and comfy armchairs. So much so, we made ourselves right at home, helping ourselves to a glass of *limoncello* before stepping out on the terrace. As usual, Fausto didn't hesitate to get straight to the point; or, as I suppose they might say around his parts, he wanted to *carpe diem* before the day was through. *"Can I stay with you tonight, my angel?"* Tossing him a sly look, I told him I was afraid he would never ask. Leave it to the practical American manager to spoil the most romantic moment of my life with my ridiculous addendum: "But with the traffic in Rome, how will you ever get to your office in time in the morning?" Thankfully, he remained faithful to his *Latin Lover* ways: *"Non preoccuparti amore mio, ci penso io—Don't worry, my love, I will deal with dat when the time comes."* We went up to the ninth floor, practically falling straight into our soft, luscious bed decked out with dozens of puffy pillows and crisp Italian linens. We stayed together all night long kissing, cuddling and bonding in a way that it seemed I had only read about in books. It was the most romantic night of my life.

The Wild Country

The next morning we awoke locked in an embrace to a beautiful, sunny day. Fausto told me he had a surprise for me—he would be taking me to see his country house. So that's how Italians 'deal with' rush hour traffic. They just skip town. Situated about 45 minutes outside of Rome, he would prepare a barbecue there and we could spend the day relaxing in the countryside. So after breakfast, we headed out to the Sabine hills and to a small village called *Poggio San Lorenzo*. This was the area near Rome that the Romans ultimately conquered back in ancient times. In fact, museums around the world carry masterworks depicting the massacre and consequent *Rape of the Sabine Women*. Approaching this quiet, picturesque, and wildly verdant part of Latium, nothing could have been further from the violence that capitulated their people to the will of the Roman Emperors.

We stopped for a coffee in the village that almost on cue offered quaint scenes of lazy summer days, reminiscent of Norman Rockwell had he been Italian. There were boys playing *calcio* or soccer in the streets, and it seemed all the old men were outdoors playing cards in the middle of the *piazza* or town square. A tidy row of old women, all wearing slightly different versions of the widow's black dress, sat along a bench, busily chatting to each other like there was not a care in the world. I couldn't help think of the sheer simplicity of their existence, a universe away from my hectic life in the advertising world. The contrast between city and countryside could not have been more conspicuous.

We set out for the local butcher's shop to buy meat for the barbecue. A hefty woman wearing a flowered housedress cum apron, a hallmark of Italian country housewives, served the customers. Her husband, wearing a bloodstained apron, sliced up and divvied out the ham, *prosciutto* and a variety of other meats at the cutting wheel. Women elbowed each other for a prime view of the prime rib. Upon leaving with our meats, all wrapped up in a tidy paper gift-wrapped package, Fausto broke into song. He started in with a verse from "*La donna ciccia*—The chubby woman—*who dons perfume of salsiccia*—sausage." I burst out in peals of laughter and made him sing me—and translate—the entire tune right on the spot.

Fausto's family home was not far from the little town square. Right upon arrival, he went into a frenzy of motion, preparing a barbecue for two, all the while chatting about how much he liked

54

to play cards, just like those men in their A-shirts sitting in the *piazza*. *"You know the only way that I can get fired from Alitalia is if they catch me playing cards in my office?"* What would become quite a common occurrence in the course of getting to know Fausto, a look of bewilderment crossed my face. I would have to get used to Fausto's Cheshire Cat ways of putting even the most basic concepts. He continued: *"I mean, eet is written in my contract dat if tey discover I am playing Briscola o Scopa in my office, they can t(h)row me away."* I didn't know what was more outrageous about that last statement. The fact that he meant they could fire him, or the fact that he might be in danger of playing a game of cards with his coworkers. I recalled my Italian grandmother playing the card game *Briscola* with her friends when I was a child, but I didn't know what *Scopa* was. I had my Italian dictionary with me and quickly looked up the word, which means, 'to sweep.' I wondered why a company would ever fire someone for sweeping the floor. Turns out, *Scopa* is just another card game but I would only learn later the vernacular of the word *scopa* means 'to screw.' Now *that* might be just cause for firing.

We ate a simple and truly scrumptious lunch of Italian sausages wrapped in sage leaves and veal cutlets in the garden, surrounded on all sides by an olive grove. It was sheer bliss. Always so generous, Fausto offered me the larger cutlet and loaded up my plate with more food than I could ever have managed. If this were to keep up, I knew I would have to get used to the Italians and their ways with food. Growing up, meals were never so protein rich, nor plates so heaped with delicacies. My dad, with the excuse that he was always on a diet, would insist on eating steak as a part of his regime. Sitting around the table, we would watch him closely, all of us drooling at the bit while he cut into his juicy T-bone steak. After polishing it off, he would gift the bone to whoever had been exceptionally good that day. The day I received my very first paycheck I bought myself a huge steak and a gallon of ice cream—my favorite flavor, chocolate-chip.

The idyllic landscape of the Sabine hills was something I had never seen before. Lazing away underneath the noonday sun, I could tell I was falling even harder for Fausto, if that could have been humanly possible. After lunch, we sipped some luscious *limoncello* liqueur while he took me around to see his olive trees and the apple orchard nearby. By way of introduction, he informed me that the apple orchard was the place where all the family pets were buried. Pointing over to one corner of the lot, in his melodramatic way he said, *"Dees is da mausoleum of da Mezzana family animals..."* I wasn't sure if it would be an awkward moment to let out an abrupt laugh. He went on to tell me their histories. The family animals were mostly birds—for the record, they were the only pets allowed *inside* the house, as long as they were kept behind bars. The other graves were for his brother's dogs—adopted long after leaving the family home—and naturally, kept out of doors. If I'd been paying closer attention, I could have concluded then and there that Italians have a very strained relationship with four-legged creatures. Later on, I would grasp just how uncanny it was that his poor pets had received a proper burial at all. After our walk, we nodded off to sleep in the garden. By the time I woke up, Fausto had already cleared the table, washed the dishes and was simply sitting there, gazing at me. *"Don't you people ever sleeep in Kalee-fornia?!"*

He then broached the subject of how we would be able to continue seeing each other. Providing his own solution to the conundrum, and channeling Cicero, the great Roman orator, he declared that he would like to give me a *"beeg prrezant"* if I would accept it. He told me that he would be able to offer me the option to fly anywhere in the world for almost nothing. It was a perk he might be able to pull off as an employee with Alitalia. It would certainly solve the problem of carrying on a long distance romance. *"What do you teenk my love? We could meet alf-way between Kali-fornia and Roma and be able to see each udder at least every seex weeks."* He continued unfolding his grand scheme, which clearly he had masterminded during my slumber. Eventually, if I were listed as his "partner" I would be able to fly anywhere across the globe under the same conditions as an Alitalia employee. I couldn't believe my ears. *"As soon as I can, I weel send you a teeket. And den you could meet me in Mee-ami...We could meet in Mee-ami in six weeks, and den fly to Santo Domingo together...What do you teenk, my love?"* My eyes widened. This wasn't just some spur of the moment pipe dream. Clearly, he had been thinking long and hard about how he could make this work, just like I had done. Not yet cognizant of the fact that I risked being fired for far worse than over a hand of cards, I contemplated my newfound status as an Alitalia jetsetter. Overjoyed, I replied, "Why not?" At this juncture in my life, I had nothing to lose (well, other than my job). It had been such a long time since meeting someone that made my heart pound; it had been years, really. And as far as my past was concerned, even my ex-husband was chopped liver at best. And although I still couldn't tell if Fausto was a genuine, genteel, grounded guy, or just another red herring in a lifetime of bad catches, he seemed like a dream come true. But before I could say one word more, up leapt frenetic Fausto from his chair, exclaiming enthusiastically, "*Okay... Andiamo!*" 'Let's go,' I thought. I didn't know if he meant back home to Rome or that we needed to get a move on to make our flight plans for the future.

Fausto's reasoning brought me straight back to the present. He innocently asked how much vacation time I had left this year. When I told him "No more days," he almost fell out of his chair. I explained that I had already used them all up between this very trip and my last fateful trip to Italy with my mom. "*Whataaaa??!! But ow ees possible that you can rest in only two weeks per year? Do you know the doctors say you need at least two weeks all together in order to be able to relaaxxx your body, your mind, your soul...??!!*" I hesitated to ask how many days he had for vacation. Now it was my turn to be flabbergasted. He had eight weeks off per year, plus all the Italian holidays...which he then started riddling off, as if knowing each and every day would ease my temporal pain: "*You know, we have Ferragosto* [The Assumption of the Virgin each August 15th], *the day off for Saints Pietro e Paolo* (Peter and Paul) *the Patron Saints of Rome, the Immacolata* [Festival of the Immaculate Conception], *La Festa della Repubblica* [the founding of the country as a Republic and the disbanding of the monarchy just after WWII], *and many more religious holidays... So, in tutto, I probably have around ten weeks or more!*" Now I understood why Italians always seemed so relaxed and appeared to enjoy their lives far more than we Americans did. Fausto then decided to elucidate me on the fundamental difference between Americans and Italians: "*You know, to be (h)appy in Italy, eet is enough you (h)ave your own car, your small apartment, and that you can go to a nice restaurant for lunch on Sunday. If you have a little more money, we go to ski for two weeks and of course we must have our t(h)ree weeks at the seaside in August. Don't you agree my love? I mean how can youra boss ever expect you to relaaxxx in just two weeks dah entire year long?"*

Thinking about my three days off—*or else*—ultimatum, I heaved a heavy sigh, cognizant that it was only another two days before I had to get back to the rat race. With it, I vowed to make sure they lasted longer than 24 hours, each one. I must have looked fairly glum over my quick prognosis because Fausto immediately chimed in to cheer me up: *"I see dat you are a bit destroyed my love."* [I would soon come to note that he would use the word 'destroyed' for almost everything bad that came his way—to my English-language ears, it sounded so totally over-the-top, but admittedly, in this instance, it rang true enough, indeed.] *"Tomorrow...I weell come to the (h)otel and we weell relax all da day by da pool."* Adding, for good measure, *"And you can sleep all da day."* Hearing his reassuring words, I started feeling a bit less *"destroyed,"* my spirits lifting on hearing he would take time off so we could have another whole day together—just the two of us.

Our day was sheer bliss. We spent our time making love between dips in the swimming pool and glorious five-star meals. We'd get dressed, start kissing passionately, get undressed again and then start all over again. As he so accurately predicted, I did fall asleep in the room. I awoke to find Fausto looking like a sexy *Lawrence of Arabia* wrapped in a towel with my black and white sarong around his head. I half-expected a Cobra snake to come dancing devilishly out of the wastebasket. We baked in the hot Roman sun and he taught me how to play *Briscola*. We spoke of our dreams and the things we wished we had or hadn't accomplished in our lives. I devoted most of my banter rooting for answers to the burning question as to why, at the age of 45, a gorgeous and gallant man like Fausto was still single. *"Well, you know, my love, I had many long relationships; one for six years, one for four. But they always wanted to put the chain on me...and I felt deep down they were not the right one."* Naturally, his dramatic claims begged the question... "What do you mean, exactly, by 'the chain?'" I teased. "Is it because you turn into a wild animal so they have to chain you up at night?" Refusing to take the bait, he sensibly carried on: *"Well, you see...dey all wanted to get married. I call it a chain, because they wanted commitment and security and I felt as I would be chained to someone—you know just like an animal in da zoo."* I should have guessed—he would be transformed into an animal regardless. Chuckling over his silly metaphors, I thought I could live like this forever. But then again, would he come to feel that *I* was a ball and chain wrapped firmly around his ankles?

That night, the hotel's general manager invited us to dine at not only the finest restaurant in Rome, but arguably in all of Italy. An evening at the *Cavalieri Hilton's* own 3-star Michelin restaurant, *La Pergola*, was awaiting us and we were salivating at the bit just thinking about our meal to come. Entering the restaurant, we were escorted up to the rooftop and handed two glasses of bubbly *prosecco* to enjoy while our table was being prepared. We were seated to start our fantasy dinner with an appetizer of king prawns in tempura on a purée of fried squids. I was relishing the exquisite prawns melting in my mouth when I looked over at Fausto and saw that he didn't seem to be savoring them as much as I. Was it due to his latent phobia for killer fish? Trying to read his thoughts, I caught him nervously checking the prices displayed on the menu over and over again, growing more anxious by the item. Finally, he let his fears be known: *"Are you shoore we are being invited tonight? Maybe you didn't understand completely."* I assured him that the invite was in English and I understood that language perfectly well. With that, he seemed to relax as he dove in to finish his prawns.

The next dish that arrived, our first course or *primo piatto* presented by two adorable twin waiters, gave both of us room for pause. We were served a tangerine *risotto* with scampi *carpaccio* and mint. While debating whether or not to give the tangy *risotto* the benefit of the doubt (decidedly <u>not</u> my favorite dish), I thought I better throw interception with Fausto's fear of yet more sea creatures. I told him to look around—surely there was no one here at *La Pergola* who may be trying to knock us off; though I'm sure the general manager might be more pleased to see me dining here alone, if he got my drift. Once successfully through our *primo*, we decided to skip the *secondo piatto* or main entrée and settled on a heavenly death-by-chocolate dessert instead. Served with a fine selection of port wines, we split it so we didn't keel straight over from caloric shock. As we headed back to the room, we giggled that even if we died that night, it didn't matter; it was an absolutely perfect repast to complete what, all in all, had been a life lived in vivid color.

We resolved over our meal that perhaps it would be better for him to come and visit me in San Diego, given my serious deficiency of vacation time. Fausto said he really wanted to see me in my own home environment; meet my friends, my family and see my life. In fact, he would plan to come and visit me in six weeks' time. For both of us, six weeks seemed to be the longest time frame we could possibly fathom being apart; anything more than that would be out of the question for either of us. Thinking about presenting him to most of my family back in San Diego, my thoughts drifted back to my big sister after she had fallen in love for the very first time. She had decided to take a trip up north from our home in Texas to introduce her boyfriend to her friends and family back home. Upon arrival, and while they were still sitting in my dad's driveway, they were met by my dad's own homegrown Welcoming Committee—a couple of thugs wielding a baseball bat. Thankfully for Fausto, my brothers were much more hands off when it came to my affairs of the heart. Come to think of it, I could think of a few choice exes I would have loved for them to have roughed up along the way, starting with the most recent one.

The next morning, Fausto showered trying not to wake me as he got ready for his day at the office. I got up anyway and decided to hide his Neapolitan playing cards; telling him it was to ward off any risk of him losing his job. We would need all the help from Alitalia we could get if we were going to see this relationship through. I spent the day between relaxing by the pool and checking emails. After work, Fausto took me over to *Villa Ada*, another beautiful park where we took a long run together. Returning to the hotel, we got ready for dinner. He told me he wanted to take me to his favorite seafood restaurant. I complimented him for living dangerously. We barreled down the mountain, Pat Metheny blaring and the rooftop open. The more time I spent with Fausto, the more I felt as though I were in a movie; this time, *The Talented Mr. Ripley*. As we sat down at our table, he told me that this was the same restaurant where he brought his parents to celebrate the closing on his apartment.

Fausto's favorite haunt is the *Taverna Cestia*, not far from the Circus Maximus and the United Nations FAO-Food & Agricultural Organization. So that explained the numerous non-Italians seated around us. As we were waiting for our food to come, Fausto leaned over as if revealing a State secret: *"You see dat table in da corner? Can you understand dat dey are your fellow countrymen?"* I looked over, and while mulling over the fact that I had pretty much never heard the phrase 'fellow countrymen' in all my 39 years, I said, "Well, no, I can't tell and besides, how can you recognize them if you haven't even heard them speak?" *"I have been watching them—da man with da blue shirt put parmigiano cheese on his seafood pasta dish and da woah-man is drinking a cappuccino at 11 o'clock!"* I cracked a smile at his astonishment over these culinary transgressions. Fausto deadpanned, *"And they are both wearing gym shoes out to dinner."* Ugh—leave it to the Ugly Americans to stand out in a crowd.

Taking his Sherlock Holmes summation for certain fact, and always eager to meet and greet any American I can find on my travels, I struck up a conversation with them just as they were leaving the restaurant. Naturally, Fausto had nailed it; they were visiting from New Jersey. While we chatted, I could see Fausto giving me the *'Here she goes again'* look. In just our short time together, he had already picked up on the fact that I would always go for that American connection, readily conversing to complete strangers no matter where I was. He couldn't complain—if he hadn't made small talk with me, we wouldn't even be sitting in this terrific *trattoria* just about now, besides. On our way back to the hotel, I couldn't help but think that by this time tomorrow I'd be leaving my little corner of *paradiso* to fly back home to perdition. I tried my best to keep in mind that I would be seeing Fausto just six and a half weeks later.

Finally, my three blissful days in Rome, which at this point seemed more like all of three hours, had drawn to an end. Fausto took me to the airport and we said our goodbyes. Never had I been so happy, nor felt so distraught, or rather, *destroyed*, by someone like this in my life. As he said his last goodbye, he called out *"Buon Viaggio bombetta mia!"* I called out after him, "But what is a *bombetta?!"* *"Oh, it is too difficult to explain now, but it means you are my leettle cream-filled donut bomb."*

For the second time in practically as many months, the whole way home I rehashed our bubbling banter, our passionate lovemaking, our intense camaraderie over and over again in my head. Fausto's peculiar observations about almost everything filled me with sheer joy. And for the first time in a very long time, in an even longer line of faulty men, I could look at the future with optimism and a sense of truly being loved. I had come full circle: Fausto was not your average fountain hanger, by now I was absolutely certain. I was looking forward to carrying on a cross-continent relationship with this idiosyncratic man. With all these good feelings floating to the surface, I was nevertheless stricken with *ansia*—anxiety of Faustian proportions. How could I so much as face my mom who was waiting for me at home and confess just what the future may hold? She had just moved all her worldly belongings from Tucson to San Diego just to be closer to me and my siblings who had migrated there over the years. Would this love affair signify that there would come a day that I would move *away* from her? I was destroyed just thinking about the consequences. As I drifted off to sleep, I vowed to take it just one day at a time. After all, Rome wasn't built in a day.

CHAPTER VI

❦

Mork & Mindy

I arrived home the next day to find my mother and stepfather sitting at my kitchen table. They had been looking after Thelma & Louise, my two Siamese kitties. My mom took one look at me and remarked, "Oh, no…I think we will lose her to Italy…" As curious as my cats, she tried to ask ever so casually, and not doing a good job of masking her fascination, how it had all gone just the same. I told her that the whole trip had been absolutely *magnifico*, front to finish, and that I would fill her in on all the juicy details the next night over dinner.

Each morning following my return from our 72-hour date was like Christmas day. I would sit down at my desk, cup of coffee in hand, open my computer and read an entire bibliography of Fausto's farcical emails sent out each evening before he left his office.

"Another assassination attempt at Roma restaurant last night—this time with oysters. T(h)anks god I am alive, baci (kisses)"

63

"Waking up without you is like having my cappuccino without the cornetto (croissant)"

Reading his missives and laughing right out loud, I thanked—or was it tanked?—my lucky stars I worked from home. Had anyone been listening in, I am sure they would have seriously wondered what was going on by now. I may not be playing cards, but in any serious office, my antics would have been cause for dismissal. Separated by a nine-hour time difference, I would answer his emails during the day, so that he would get them either that evening, or the next morning when he got back to work.

After three dreamy days on top of the world, it wasn't easy to return to my routine existence as it had been pre-Fausto. I felt as though I had been transported from a Technicolor ancient Oz, back to a black and white version of my humdrum life. Although my days always ran at a frenetic pace, I had always regarded San Diego as a terrific place to be. But suddenly, everything looked drab and different compared to Rome. Compared to Rome with Fausto. Compared to Fausto. The next six weeks would not be a stroll in the park, but we survived with emails, letters, and hours spent burning up the phone lines.

Fausto finally arrived at the San Diego airport and would be staying for seven days. I met him at Arrivals, toting a poster that read, *Fausto for President*. He got a big kick out of my homemade sign with his blown up photograph plastered on it. His unbridled enthusiasm was as contagious as I had remembered. He told me that he got through customs carrying as much of *buonissima* and *bellissima* Italy as he positively could manage. In fact, his bags were bursting with smooth bricks of *parmigiano* cheese, lemony *limoncello*, large cakes of *panettone*, and every other Italian delicacy he knew I loved and couldn't get in San Diego. He had also tried to smuggle in ten different types of salami, enough to stage a smorgasbord representing every region of Italy. Unfortunately for all of us, it had been confiscated in short order immediately upon arrival. Relating how he watched the agricultural authorities toss it carelessly into a sanitary bin, Fausto cried out that he had been thoroughly *robbed*—by the airport personnel themselves.

Although overjoyed to see me, he remarked he was completely *"destroyed"* by the long flight. But by now, I knew not to worry and, more importantly, to tell *him* not to worry—he could go and take a nap as soon as we got home. Back at the house, Thelma & Louise greeted us at the door. Each sized up the other curiously with Fausto delivering a line of questioning not unlike Little Red Riding Hood and her dear wolf. Although he made a valiant attempt at masking his curiosity by inquiring about the breed, I soon realized he was aiming to glean their medical histories and teeth size to boot.

"Dair orecchi (ears) *look like volves they are so beeg and not like any other cats I have ever seen."*

"Dey are looking at me like I am dee exotic animal."

"Do you think eet ees eeh-genick that they stay in the house?"

To wit, I had to ask what, exactly, he meant by hygienic. Clearly, the cats were making him quite uneasy. I surmised that he was worried about catching some rare and god-awful disease. "They're *indoor* cats," I said reassuringly, miffed that we were even having such a conversation. "They *never* go out," I admonished, thinking that that quite settled the question of communicable diseases in house cats. Although it struck me as a peculiar comment at the time, I would understand only much later that there wasn't an Italian worth all the salt in the Mediterranean who was ever quite comfortable with the unbridled attachment Americans had to their pets.

I had a small meal waiting for him. He was especially grateful for it, although I was quite certain it didn't come even spitting distance to the Italian meals he was used to eating; especially those prepared by his *mamma* on a regular basis. Of course, it didn't come close to the meals I had been raised on, either. Growing up, we had one small dining table that naturally did not accommodate the lot of us. So we ate in shifts. We kids would be served up some heap of potatoes or rice or other filling substance to get us through our days. On nights my dad would play a gig, he'd come home very late bringing a deep dish Chicago pizza pie underarm. He would proceed to wake us all up just so he wouldn't have to eat it alone; well, he'd have us drowsy kids for company, but he'd still eat the entire pie all by himself—We'd watch him devour it with gusto, our mouths watering, even in our sleep-induced haze.

After dinner, all four of us fell fast asleep. Fausto and I snuggling together, Thelma & Louise cuddled at our feet. But at about 4:00 in the morning, I awoke to find Fausto nervously pacing the house. Naturally, I chalked it up to a case of jetlag. Instead, Fausto said somewhat apologetically that he didn't want to wake me up but that he had been unable to sleep. Appearing slightly agitated, he did venture to probe if I always slept with Thelma & Louise. "Of course!" I replied carelessly, not understanding that perhaps therein lay the crux of the matter. *"Well, your bed is a bit like dee Serengeti safari park."* In my stupor, I wondered where this metaphor would be taking us. He related to me that ever-curious Thelma had been walking across his face trying to figure out who this *"exotic animal"* was, as he would refer to himself on occasion. Only at the start of our cross-cultural and cross-continental relationship, and we had already hit upon our first big challenge of staying together as a couple. Domestic animals, that we Americans consider pets and part of the family, Italians regard as filthy, flea-ridden beasts of burden.

It's not like Fausto wasn't used to having cats around. In fact, Rome is famous for its cat colonies; thousands of cats in every shape, size and coloring parading the streets, romping in the forum, and stretching out on just about every surface bathed in sun. Unfortunately for me, it is a rare occurrence to find a Roman cat cohabiting with the Romans indoors. For a hypochondriac like Fausto, Thelma nosing up to him in his sleep was pretty muck akin to rubbing his face in a plague-infested pillowcase. I could see this was not going to be an easy issue to surmount, and certainly not in the middle of the night. I tried to convince him that Thelma was just curious and she just needed a bit more time to get used to him. That explanation fell sorrowfully flat. By this time, it was clear that this particular impasse undoubtedly would take longer to overcome than just one evening. Getting up to put Thelma outside the door, I managed to convince Fausto to come back to bed. Eyeing Louise with suspicion, he finally dozed off after his jetlag got the better of him; the three of us sleeping soundly, right in a row like the three little pigs. The next morning we discovered that while we were deep in slumber, Thelma had exacted her revenge on this rude intruder—by peeing in his suitcase.

After breakfast together, I reminded Fausto that I needed to get started on work because I didn't have any more vacation time for a long while. He asked if he could take my bicycle and go for a ride down to the beach. I said that sounded like a great idea—seeing that I had a conference call and then a few other errands to run as well. So, off he went like a knight into battle, his charge, *"Okay, I go!"* We would see each other later. He took off out the back door and on his way. He was still out and about when I left to run my errands, unwittingly locking the door behind me out of force of habit. A few hours later, I came home to find Fausto lounging on my back terrace. He informed me that he had been unable to get in the house. I was aghast. I asked how long he had been waiting, and he said, *"Oh, only for a couple of (h)ours."* *Mamma mia!* I could tell we were off to a really banner start.

That evening, we decided to meet my good friend, Kali, for drinks. I wanted to show off my 'exotic animal' and I wanted to show off my city to him. Dashing as always, Fausto ordered a martini. But when his drink arrived, he stared at it strangely, totally perplexed. I thought maybe he was wondering if it was poisoned. He then said that it was not what he had ordered, and that he had asked for a martini. I countered that it *was* a martini, imploring him to just go ahead and try it. He took one sip and a look of sheer abomination came over his face. Still trying to maintain composure, he politely said, *"No, my love, this is terreeball!"* And with a start, Fausto shot up and went directly behind the bar. Now I was the one who was unglued. I watched bemused as he pointed out to the bartender a bottle with the words *Martini&Rossi* written upon it. Running up after him, I offered by way of explanation to both him and the bartender that if he orders a martini in America, his drink would be what he first received—a concoction of vodka and vermouth, topped with an olive. Like the ad always suggested, he'd have to ask for *Martini&Rossi* by name.

Our entire courtship would be peppered by these *Mork&Mindy* moments. Most of the time, Fausto would leave us both howling with glee. Sitting back down at the oceanfront bar, Fausto started telling us about the time he went scuba diving with his friend, Antonio. He told us how much he loved diving but the last time he went, they tested him and his friend before venturing out to sea. *"Pointing to me, the dive master said…'Okay, you can' and pointing at my frraind, Antonio 'you doesn't can!'"* Kali and I just dissolved into laughter over his grammatical *faux pas*. Only once I started taking Italian lessons did I understand how Fausto would translate literally from Italian to English and really, how difficult it was to speak two very different languages. Needless to say, right from the martini episode onward, he kept us in stitches the entire evening.

The next day, my mother came over for breakfast. The two of them carried on like a pair of old friends from high school. She laughed for hours, confiding to me how happy she was to see him again; as if I had as much as a modicum of doubt. That evening, I organized an early birthday party, inviting my closest friends and family. My twin sister and I always celebrated our birthday together, so that morning we went out and ordered a huge cake for the both of us. By nightfall, Fausto had my entire group of 'fountain hanger' friends eating out of the palm of his hand. Playing charades, Fausto got the movie, *Hush, Hush Sweet Charlotte* to act out. He spent the next ten minutes trying to have us guess the word 'Charlotte' by pointing over and over to the leftover birthday cake. We guessed everything from the film *16 candles* to *Chocolat*. Even my sister, Renee, who has worked her entire life in Hollywood, couldn't come up with the answer. After we effectively had all given up, he blurted out, *"My God, don't you have dee Charlotte cake in America?!"* We drew a collective blank.

The evening came to an abrupt end after my sister's dog bit my brother's leg while he was pounding on the cement of my back terrace for the clue to *A Streetcar Named Desire*. Fausto, in Emergency Room mode, ran into the house immediately. I was convinced he'd be right back with a tourniquet for my brother and a tranquilizer gun for the dog. Instead, out he came armed with a bowl of ice wrapped in a towel and a bottle of *limoncello*. Handing a glass over to Jimmy, he declared that in times like these, enough *limoncello* would kill any pain. My brother drank down almost the entire bottle. From that point on, Fausto nicknamed my brother *Limoncello* and his son, *Limoncellino* (little *limoncello*).

It had been an incredibly fun evening for all. My friends phoned the next day to say how much they enjoyed meeting Fausto. They could tell just how much he cared about and loved me, and the best part was, they told me he had been promoted from fountain hanger to official boyfriend. They were all very happy for me. My family found him to be highly entertaining and officially welcomed him into the family with their brand of teasing and ribbing, which for the Tondelli clan is a sure sign of affection.

After work and weekends were spent at the beach. One day on the beach, after I decided that the Serengeti Park incident was well enough behind us, I needed to know more about Fausto's economic situation. I started drilling him with all the right questions about his finances. "How much debt do you have?" "How much do you owe on credit cards?" "How much is your mortgage?" It would be quite an understatement to state that Fausto was taken aback. *"What kind of strange questions are you asking me, my love?"* Bewildered, and most likely not expecting such a straightforward line of questioning, especially from a romantic interest, he said, *"I don't understand why you are so interreasted in deese teengs."* By way of explanation, I recounted to him that my last partner, whom I had pretty stupidly ended up marrying, had sold me a bill of goods that were bogus at best. My ex had related that he owned lots of stocks and shares in companies, and that he was highly financially stable. It was only after we were married that I discovered, in reality, he owed thousands upon thousands of dollars in credit card debt, and his million dollars of shares were worth nothing. By marrying me, not only did I provide a house for him to live in, but also I would be responsible for his debts. Adding insult to injury, he never did come clean on his actual situation. Like getting broadsided by a Mack Truck, I had found all this out the hard way: opening up one of his credit card statements. And to think, what I had discovered on a single line item had been just the tip of the iceberg.

I beat myself up for being such a fool then. *Fool me once, shame on you. Fool me twice, shame on me.* When I stopped to think about it, incredibly, my dad had gone and done the same to my mom. For years, he neglected to pay the tax or social security payments for his band members. The lenders finally put a lien on the house. When he sold our house and shipped us out to Texas, he claimed that all the money from the sale had gone to the bankers. From where I was today, I'm quite certain that he simply pocketed the difference and my mother was never the wiser. At least, when I finally unraveled the web of deceit and it was my turn to dump the bum, I had only two cats to care for, and not a brood of children to look after besides.

Reassuring me that he was not this type of guy, Fausto emphatically stated that he only had a couple of hundred dollars on credit cards. In actual fact, Italians are the greatest savers in the world. And at the time, only 1% of the population even used credit cards; so it was no wonder why he thought my queries were *"So strange questions, my love."* For my part, and although it was no guarantee, I still felt I had to ask. And although I had to take his reply at face value, I was truly relieved to learn he was financially mature. Despite these hiccups, we made it successfully to the end of our seven days in cross-cultural training. I felt that we had turned a page on another phase of our relationship. By this time, I felt confident about our future and my financial future; if what he said was true, in the very least, I would not end up paying off credit card debt incurred by fiery Fausto.

Our last night together I wanted to make the mood just right for a romantic Italian dinner at home. So I started in, lighting candles all over the house. This simple gesture set Fausto, usually an incurable romantic, straight into a tailspin. For him, candles were an undeniable method to make sure that the house would burn down right to the ground. Perhaps Romans have an innate fear of fire from their history, when Rome was devastated from fire under Emperor Nero. But all I know is that while I was busy preparing dinner, Fausto busied himself combing the house to snuff out half the candles; convinced in his zealotry that he was saving us from surefire disaster.

Setting out to prepare the perfect meal, I knew that I couldn't just toss some rigatoni in boiling water and open some marinara sauce from a jar. Italians are extremely particular about their pasta. They treasure their food and it has to be as good as *mamma* makes. For an American, even one who had our Italian grandmother practically living in our home, this was a daunting task. By the end of my culinary endeavor I was a nervous wreck. I set out making a lovely *puttanesca* sauce of fresh tomatoes, basil, olives and anchovies. Of course, Fausto was eager to provide his own brand of commentary on my fine food selection: I discovered that *puttanesca* literally means 'like a prostitute;' basically, a sauce made with red pepper, it's considered a 'very hot dish.' The more time I spent with Fausto, the evermore convinced I was that almost everything in Italy boils down to food, animals or sex.

Finally, our seven-day full immersion course in cross-cultural relationships was up, and we kissed madly at the airport and said our goodbyes. Fausto left saying, *"Goodbye, my love—see you in six weeks in Santo Domingo."* Our midway point between North America and the Old Continent—in more ways than one.

CHAPTER VII

❧

Six and a Half Weeks

It was decided: immediately following Fausto's departure, I would embark on an intensive program of Italian lessons. This was important if I ever wanted to carry on a normal conversation with anyone in his world. Neither his mother and father spoke a word of English, nor did the majority of his friends, nor, come to think of it, did most of his extended family for that matter. I hoped to impress him with my newfound linguistic abilities when we would next see each other, in six weeks' time in Santo Domingo. We had decided on Santo Domingo for its nearly perfect climate and the fact that it was about equidistant from both San Diego and Rome. It helped that it was filled with luxurious resorts where we could just relax in each other's company; no friends, no family, no furry creatures, no further distractions, just the two of us in the company of perfect strangers. Little did we know that left to our own devices, even those outsiders would run interference in our holiday extravaganza.

Selecting the resort in Santo Domingo, Fausto related that we'd be *"Spending five bellissimi days, just for each other."* I couldn't argue with this: Fausto had made it his personal mission to make sure at least one American enjoyed life to the fullest, job security be damned. It sounded sublime, albeit less so after I learned he had signed me up for scuba diving lessons. This fantasy island package had only one glitch (well, two, if you counted the scuba diving): It was October, and I had no more vacation time until the following April. What could I do? Practicing some of that Italian finesse at beating the system, I concocted my escape plan. I would tell my boss that I was deathly ill, take three workdays off, and have the weekend with Fausto to boot. As long as my boss didn't see me with a sun-kissed face and a sensational tan, I thought I might actually get away with it. To *"leeve my dreams,"* as Fausto would say, meaning, to "live out my dreams," not leave them behind like some old forgotten handbag. Being able to count on a home office helped seal the deal—I just might get away with playing hooky in paradise. Besides, it was a risk worth taking if I wanted this relationship to go any further than a few sumptuous *gelati* and beyond a few glasses of luscious *limoncello*.

I felt gypped. Why was it that in every other country the world over people had so much time off to enjoy their life, while we Americans were so intent on making sure we put more face time in at the office? The biggest challenge in our relationship would not be the intrusion of Siamese cats in the bed. It would be the intrusion of labor hours into perfectly valuable R&R time. Maybe we could all learn something from this culture that really knew how to enjoy life. In Italian, they call it *'dolce far niente'* —sweet do-nothing; in short, the joy of being as idle as a couch potato. Except Italians didn't fill their downtime by sitting themselves straight down on the couch; they traveled, went skiing, explored, and even learned to scuba dive. I was not only falling more and more in love with Fausto, but his entire way of seeing life, Italian-style.

Our six-week interlude seemed like an eternity. In the final stretch, I even had to endure the trial of three long days sitting through another boring business conference; this one in New York. At long last, I found myself in the Miami airport, looking for another date with Mr. Strange Destiny himself—my *bello* Fausto. We had arranged to meet there and take the flight to Santo Domingo together. Although I was to land first, my plane was delayed so I started looking out for Fausto right upon arrival. We had a seriously tight connection. Stopping a moment to rummage my bags for my phone, I felt again those familiar, soft piano-playing hands around my eyes... *"Hello, my love, welcome to Miami!"* We kissed quickly before making a mad dash for our gate. We made our plane just in the nick of time, landing two hours later in sunny Santo Domingo.

Paradise Lost

We had hired a private driver to pick us up and ferry us to our resort. We didn't see much of the Santo Domingo scenery, spending the entire car ride just kissing and holding each other. We arrived to what I thought was the closest thing to Shangri-la; a secluded place brimming with palm trees, white sandy beaches and our own private bungalow that would be our love nest for the next few days. I surveyed the scenery thinking that when it came to playing hooky, the Italians surely knew how to do it right.

After spending our first night in, we slipped off into a deep sleep. We could have been anywhere it didn't matter, as long as we were together. But at 9:00 the next morning, our tranquil slumber came to an abruptly loud end. The sounds of salsa music and merengue wafted through the air and right into our bedroom. At first I wondered if this wasn't some surprise from Fausto; I wouldn't put it past him to have ordered a mariachi band for our wake-up call. Turned out the resort offered dancing lessons each morning by the pool. "Wow!" I turned to Fausto, "I love salsa, *Andiamo!*" *"But I need my cappuccino and cornetto before I can go anywhere..."* he protested drowsily, with more than a hint of incredulity in his voice. "Okay, but do it quickly!" I shot back at him and jumped out of bed to put on some clothes as fast as I could.

Busy preparing, I recounted that as long as I could remember I was dancing. I owe my love of dance to my oldest sister, Renee, who bought me a pair of Ginger Rogers gold plastic dancing shoes when I was just three years old. They had been my most prized possession. Afternoons she would spend teaching me and my other sisters how to cha cha, tango and fox trot. Coupled with my father's musician friends always rehearsing around our house, well, I learned rhythm and movement before I could even walk. And much to Fausto's chagrin, I never missed out on an opportunity to kick up my heels.

We arrived poolside at the very moment the instructor was dividing us into groups; beginners or advanced dancers. After about five minutes of watching us dance, the instructor said to me, "You come into this group—your partner needs to go into the beginner's group." Fausto's anguish was palpable...and entirely audible as well. *"Whataaaaa??!! Oh no, my love...I am suffereeng...Eet's not pohssible dey are putting me wit all the babies!"* By this time, it was clear that for Italians, anything just beyond the confines of their comfort zone was a prime occasion for misery. It's no wonder they get the claim to fame for quality of life experiences. They can't handle anything less. But when Fausto pronounced it, I always thought he literally would keel right over. *"But I can't be a beginner..."* Unequivocally, and with no regard for his fragile Latin male ego, the instructor said, "I am sorry, *Signore*, you are not as good as she is." And they left it at that. I could feel Fausto's eyes following me as my partner, Paolo, twirled me around like a tilt-a-whirl at a carnival. At one point, I caught a glimpse of Fausto pleading his case to the salsa instructor one last time. I had to giggle when I saw Ignacio, the salsa boss, just shake his head "No." Although I felt bad for Fausto, I was having the time of my life, frolicking with the hot, sunkissed Dominican men. Besides, later that day, it'd be Fausto in the advanced group for scuba diving, and me, just a '*baby*'. And I would have to live with that. We were even, as far as I was concerned. I would learn later just how competitive Fausto was—and in hindsight, how it nearly killed him to have to suffer the humility of being cast into the beginner's group. As for Fausto, as soon as he set foot back on Roman soil, he signed up for salsa lessons so he would never have to live down that kind of public opprobrium again.

My idea of playing hooky

That afternoon I found myself in the swimming pool, covered head to toe with scuba gear and wetsuit. With the way I looked, I realized my boss would be hard-pressed to catch me with a golden tan. In fact, he could have been right here at the same resort and he wouldn't have even recognized me all dressed up like a hi-tech creature from the black lagoon. It wasn't my favorite seaside activity, but still, I was open to give it a try. Fausto came by the swimming pool where we were having our first open water lesson to offer encouragement: *"I see you are suffering my love...Don't warry, by dee end of da week we will be flying together along with the beautiful fish in da sea."* I asked if there was an easier way to fly together instead of under the water line. *"Coraggio (*have courage*) my love, you will tell me tanks, I prohmeese you."*

That evening at dinner as I helped myself to a huge salad, Fausto and his food alarm went into overdrive. Taking one look at my salad plate, with horror in his eyes, he cried out, "*What are you doing my love?!* *Do not eat dat lettuce. It is not verry (h)eegenic!*" Taking a brief inventory of all the items Fausto insisted were not healthy in his world, starting with homicidal fish, I merely shrugged my shoulders and ate it anyway. Unfortunately for me, it was payback time for Fausto. That very evening I started feeling queasy. Before the night was through, I started vomiting violently, and soon thereafter found myself in the throes of a full-blown case of Montezuma's revenge. A fever came on so strongly I thought I had contracted malaria. Even though I was the one burning hot, as soon as Fausto felt my fever coming on, it almost did him in. Fausto went into full-blown EMS paramedic panic mode.

Implementing Emergency Procedure no. 1, he first asked where I kept my *termo-meter.* I told him not only did I not even own one, but also that it certainly wouldn't have been part of my carry-on case for a trip—*anywhere.* Not one to be discouraged, he quickly followed this with, "*Okay, where then is your medicine bag?*" "My medicine bag? Do I look like a witch doctor of some sort?" Thinking what I must have looked like given my current state of affliction, "Don't answer that." Making a mad dash to the bathroom, and in a vain attempt to be a bit more compliant, I said, "Sorry, it must have gotten left behind mistakenly back in San Diego..." And with that, Fausto sprang into action like Superman as he jumps into a phone booth to change. "*Non preoccuparti!— don't warry!*" He reached into his own bag of tricks, pulled out his very own thermometer, and tucking it under my armpit, he ran out to call the nearest doctor to come to our room immediately. He needed official verification to see that I was, indeed, officially a basket case. For two full days, I could barely hoist myself out of bed much less leave the room for dining under the stars (not that I could eat anything, anyway.) Fausto attended to me like some hyperkinetic Florence Nightingale (she *was* born in Florence, Italy, after all.) He brought me all my meals, administered his vast array of medicines (in his book, clearly more being the very merrier) and coerced the doctor to visit me on a daily basis. He insisted I eat "*in bianco,*" meaning only foods that were white in color, starting the first day with only rice—the last thing I wanted in my life, healthy or not—with nothing on it. You graduate to potatoes and sometimes a drizzle of olive oil. If this regimen doesn't help you get better, you do anyway by the sole power of desperation to eat colored food again, consequences be damned. His grandma's recipe for recovery only hardened my revulsion for rice dishes, in every manner of shape, taste or form.

Every so often, I would open my eyes to see Fausto's sweet face looking down on me. He would brush the hair off my forehead and whisper softly, "*Dormi, amore, dormi—Sleep, my love, sleep.*" But all I could think of was how I spent my very own *Blue Lagoon* romance with the man whom I had been waiting for six whole weeks, 'riding the porcelain bus.' Perhaps it was God's way to pay me back for having told my boss that I was deathly ill and needed three days' bed rest. In the end, that's exactly what I got for my unabashed Santo Domingo exploit. During our *Rome-by-Night* extravaganza, Fausto had taken me over to Rome's *Castel Sant'Angelo* to point out the statue of Archangel Michael atop of it. As a symbol for all of humanity, there he was, Michael, in all his heavenly glory, sheathing his sword. Legend has it he appeared from above the mausoleum cum castle during the plague, and the act of putting away his sword was the sign that the Black Death of 590 had finally come to an end. I prayed for my own Archangel to usher in an end to my suffering. I bargained with God, vowing that from this day forward, I would never take Fausto's health precautions for granted again.

By the third day, my temperature thankfully had returned to normal, and the vomiting had finally subsided. So much for winning over your man through his stomach. I figured that if he still loved me after seeing me in this sorry condition, it would truly be a relationship worth pursuing for the long run. I supposed there was one way to test if a man loves you truly: witnessing how he reacts when you get sick. Fausto, with his manic fixation on medicating everything from a bee sting to the bubonic plague, passed that test with flying colors; red, white and green. Later, I would discover that for Italians, any sign of fever provokes unfounded fears of the flu epidemic that killed off a third of Europe at the turn of the last century. For Italians, fever is the first step toward a full-blown aviary flu or ebola virus outbreak.

Fausto in Santo Domingo trying to avoid catching
life-threatening diseases

This health-conscious (or was it sickness-conscious?) mode of living was so vastly different than how I had been raised. No illness was ever deemed too grave to do something about it. We all just learned to grin and bear it. The time my appendix had become so inflamed it was about to burst I was living in Texas with my sisters and my mom. I kept on complaining that I had a terrible tummy ache. My mom, thinking it was something I had eaten, told me to take a few aspirin and I'd be fine. As the pain worsened, she upped the ante, telling me to try some whiskey. Fortunately for me, my dad happened to walk in the front door. He had come down on a guilt trip to celebrate their 25th anniversary. He took one look at me and barked at my mother to rush me to the nearest hospital. They took out my appendix just in the nick of time. That episode notwithstanding, to this day I really could care less if I come down with something or other (food poisoning on my only three-day holiday aside). If it weren't for Fausto's remonstrations, most of my illnesses would barely register on my radar.

Finally given a clean bill of health (not by the doctor, but by Fausto, whose rubrics were much more stringent), I was able to devote the last two days to rest and relaxation—well, Fausto's version of R&R anyway—catching up on my missed scuba lessons. I even astonished myself by summoning the wherewithal to pass my diving test. We spent our last day in Santo Domingo diving together. As usual, Fausto was right: It was the closest thing to flying that I had ever experienced. Although we only had two full days of fun in the sun together, they were still two unforgettable days with the man I by now was fairly certain was *The One*. As we parted ways at the Miami airport, Fausto chirped, *"You go right, my love, and I go left…see you in da middle in six weeks…"*

Six weeks. That would make it Christmastime. It had only been five months since we had met, five deliriously joyous months. Five lifetimes ago. A wrinkle in time, really, since both of us harbored the strange suspicion that we had been together forever. Still, I yelled after him as I left his side, "What do we do for Christmas?!" *"I come to you…Ciao, my love, e Buon Viaggio!—Have a nice trip!"* Boarding the plane, I began to panic thinking how it would be humanly possible to fit Fausto in with my intense holiday work schedule. I started thinking what new story I would have to concoct in order to be with him. Actually, they'd have to be two stories: one for my boss so I am not traveling on business, and one for Fausto to explain why, over a holiday celebrating the birth of Christ, Americans still had to put in time at the office. Not for the first time I spent a plane ride questioning America's vacation-challenged system. If this were to keep up, our relationship would most certainly turn into one of Fausto's dramatic "*tragedies.*"

Christmas Vacation

As promised, Fausto did manage to come to San Diego for Christmas. Seeing his face all lit up with joy at seeing me at the airport, I could not bring myself then, nor once we were at home, to break the news that I'd even be working on Christmas Eve. In the end it would be a moot point. Fausto had his own work stress to deal with. He was charged to be 'on call' for the Y2K debacle that was thought would wreak havoc upon the entire Alitalia computer systems, his area of expertise. Instead of being a few miles away in Rome in case of certain catastrophic cyber fallout, there he was, at all hours of the day or night, managing all the work arounds by phone straight from my office in San Diego. It would be the one time on record in which I wasn't the only one who had to work through the holiday season. Luckily for Fausto, Y2K was a wash and his colleagues were none the wiser. I could have just seen it had Y2K actually exploded into a real crisis how his bosses would have liked that one. This infringement would have certainly been regarded as far more serious than being caught at your work station playing a game of computer solitaire.

For Christmas, Fausto brought me a new ski suit, a pair of ski gloves and a hat. Unfortunately for him, I had to break the news that this was one city girl that didn't know how to ski. Handing me his present, he declared, "*Dees, my love, is so we two can go skiing.*" Gulp. First scuba diving, now skiing? Talk about a man for all seasons. Knowing Fausto's penchant for serendipity, I ventured to ask, "When, exactly?" "*Dees Febuary,*" he quipped, in his totally self-assured and matter-of-fact way. I told him I had never skied in my life. Never one to let minor obstacles get in his way, and always quick with the comeback, he elucidated me with his personal recommendation for smoothly sailing down the slopes: *"Eets eazzy...You must learn to hate (h)air."* "Hate, who, exactly?" *"Dee mountain."* Well, if it's so easy, why did visions of *Joe Versus the Volcano* come to mind? He told me not to worry—he would teach me to ski, just like I had taught him to dance salsa. Now it was my turn for an onslaught of anxiety. I had a sneaking suspicion this next trip would be as successful as our last one—except instead of being stuck in a hotel room with food poisoning, I'd end up in a hospital bed in traction.

Learning to ski at 40 would be the easy part. I started stressing out over how would I manage to take off another week of work. I may have been a top earner last year, but this year, my sales targets were way off course. I may lose my job, but at least I could say I had fun doing it. And, more importantly, I had achieved one major success: flipping my *Unlucky at love—Lucky at work* dichotomy. Once again, I heard myself explaining to my hardheaded Italian our company's vacation policy. *"Va bene*—Very well," I said, "February is in six weeks. I will have to finagle getting off work for one week. Where do we meet?" *"I have already reserved a (h) otel in Selva Val Gardena...Do you know the Dolomites, my love?"* I gave him my usual American kneejerk response when asked about geographic territories, "Actually, no..." This was quickly followed by his trademark, *"What da??!! Oh—but what do you study in America?! You don't know where the Dolomites are?!"* Dejectedly, I said no, not exactly... *"I am going to send you the map of Italia—so you can study my country geography..."* I reminded him that I had already seen maps of Italy during my Italian lessons. *"Oh, my love, don't waste your time with the Italian language! I can teach you piano, piano—slowly, slowly!"* "In fact, I have my Italian lesson the day after tomorrow. Will you come with me?" *"Okay,"* he said, *"I think it will be verry entertaining..."*

After spending Christmas day together with my mom and some of my siblings, the next day we went to my lesson. Leaving the class, he said he felt much like an *"exotic animal"* in there, and couldn't help but smile throughout the entire experience. Here we were, twelve of us trying our hardest to pronounce *'porto le ciabatte'*—I am wearing my slippers. How ridiculous we must have sounded. Turns out, my teacher was spot-on. Italians never migrate one inch in the house without slippers between their feet and the floorboards. We rang in the new millennium at the La Jolla Hyatt, celebrating with my two sisters, Renee and Christine, dancing and drinking champagne; ringing in a new century, a new life and truly a new beginning. Sadly, before I knew it, there we were again, back at the airport, with Fausto going right, and I going left. This time, I knew we would see each other again in just six more weeks, this time in the Dolomites—wherever they were.

A few days before getting ready to leave for our ski trip, Fausto called. He said that he needed to tell me something terribly important. My heart absolutely sank. The pit in my stomach grew two sizes—just like the Grinch's heart. I took a deep breath, thinking, "Okay, here it comes...he has a wife and a couple of kids, a house with a dog maybe even two cats of his own who crawl across his face at night..." As cool as I could, I asked, "What is it that you need to tell me?" *"Well, before we leave for the Dolomeetay, I need to ask you someting verrry important. I would like to make the official presentation of you to my entire family."* "Official presentation? *Whatdaaa??!!"* In my mind, an 'official presentation' always meant a sales presentation with a tidy powerpoint show. I wasn't quite sure how I'd come off as Exhibit A. *"In Italy,"* Fausto continued, *"the official presentation to da family means that you are verrry serious wit someone, and dat usually it means you will eventually marry the woman you take (h)ome to meet your parents."* I couldn't determine if I were more anxious over meeting his parents or for his broadsiding me with the insinuation of a marriage proposal. In retrospect, I never fully grasped the importance of this occasion for an Italian citizen. But what I did know was that despite the miles and months between us, ours was evolving into a much more serious relationship than just a terrific vacation for two every six weeks. I said okay, and he said that I should pack something nice to wear for the presentation dinner. Still unsure how he would go about 'presenting' me, I said "No problem," and threw something I would wear for an important sales event into my bag.

84

Meet the Parents

"You see dat woman walking towards us wit da man wit da white hair? Dat is my mamma." I took a deep breath. Italian *mammas* were legend. *"The man with hees arm around her, dat is my papà. You will meet my entire family tonight."* I was starting to grow uneasy. I knew a thing or two about Italian *mammas*. My dad's mother, Josephine, lived near us in Chicago. She made nearly daily visits to teach us girls how to make homemade *gnocchi* or to crochet slippers, and she even owned and rented out the apartment right upstairs. Once my dad had moved half the family to Texas, he made sure he moved his mistress and future wife straight into her apartment one flight up. True to her Italian roots, '*Mà*' (as she insisted we call her) would never have dreamt to breathe so much as a word; her lips sealed as tightly as salami in its sack. While we strained ourselves trying to get to month's end without an eviction notice, her only precious *bambino* was carrying on with his girlfriend right under her nose and practically above our heads. Always the willing accomplice, my grandmother plied him with money for years—money that did not go to helping out her grandchildren. For an Italian, the *mamma* bond wasn't tied with a flimsy apron string; it was stronger than the steel girders holding up the Chicago 'L'.

We walked into the restaurant and there they were seated, Fausto's entire extended family—a dozen sets of prying eyes sizing me up all at the same time. For once, I knew what it was like to feel like the exotic animal; it was as if Fausto was seeing to it that I be presented like a peacock on a silver platter fit for a king. Gathered around the table were Fausto's parents, his brothers and their wives and children. Despite the nerves of being the absolute center of attention, I let out a great sigh of relief: Such a public outing signified that he was not harboring a secret wife and kids kept hidden in an apartment in town. Unless, of course, they were all in on the secret. One by one, they each rose to greet me warmly, with a kiss or a handshake, their thoughts resounding in my mind: "So, who was this *Americana* with an Italian last name but who didn't speak a single word of Italian?" Finally, Fausto stood up to make a toast. It was his official presentation of me, perhaps one day his future bride. Despite months of Italian lessons, I understood next to nothing. In fact, all I could remember from my Italian class was *'porto le ciabatte,'* and I seriously doubted they'd be overly impressed with "I come with slippers."

Whatever he said, it must have been good, because afterward, everyone treated me even more kindly than before. Fausto acted as my personal interpreter the entire evening. I turned on the charm, smiling a lot and talking with my hands, hoping they would understand me and get a glimpse of my personality. The meal and presentation successfully over, we went back to his parents' house for a *dopocena*—an after-dinner get-together of celebratory drinks, featuring our favorite, *limoncello*. All said and done, it had been a spectacular evening. I prayed I had passed the test and shown myself as a parent-pleaser. *'Parenti'* in Italian means 'relatives.' I hoped I had pleased all of his *parenti* in the end, but especially, his parents.

The next day, we were invited to his brother's house for another family dinner. I was starting to see firsthand that almost everything in Italy always revolved around sharing meals. Moreover, family life with the Mezzana clan appeared to me immensely tranquil. There were no uproarious voices, no kids tearing from room to room; just cordial conversation and courtesy amongst all and sundry. It was warm, welcoming, comfortable, and most importantly, Fausto's charming histrionics aside, fantastically drama-free. Even the children were remarkably well-behaved. The few times my mother and father went out for dinner, we kids would turn the house upside down and into a scene from *Animal House.* My older brothers and sisters would call their 100 closest friends, and within minutes we'd be throwing a giant frat party. My brother Joe would use us little girls for shooting practice, lining us up against a wall and taking potshots with a BB gun. Or the guys would play 'bozo buckets,' using us younger ones as bouncing balls, only to dump us into laundry baskets mercifully stuffed with dirty clothes to soften the blow.

The following day, we were off to the Dolomites, which I had discovered on Fausto's map were located somewhere near the Austrian border. I spent five days skiing each and every day: mornings, I learned technique with a cute Italian instructor who called himself Tony Macaroni; afternoons were spent practicing with Fausto by my side. After five days, although I still wasn't a very good skier, I counted myself fortunate that I had so far all my bones intact in my pursuit of four-season Italian living. Despite my good fortune, this time, it would be Fausto who would take a turn for the worse.

From Chicago city girl to Dolomites ski bunny

It came about suddenly, and over dinner, as seemed to be our tradition. While eating a delectable chocolate *soufflé a la mode*, I was regaling him with more stories about my wacky family. With so many siblings, I certainly had enough material to last a lifetime. We got onto the subject of nieces and nephews. Without batting

87

an eyelash, I related how my brother-in-law, after four children, had decided to undergo a vasectomy. Then and there, the color from Fausto's face drained completely. The Italian restaurant matron took one look at him and his pale complexion and rushed to his assistance. She helped him out of his chair and out of doors to get some fresh air. Not fully comprehending that whatever he had been stricken with was due wholly to my innocent tale, and seriously underestimating the extent of his crisis of machismo, I figured he'd be back in a few moments. So I simply continued carrying on eating my dessert. When I was finished and he hadn't yet returned, I went to look for him, eventually finding him prostrate on a couch in the lobby.

The Dolomites are pretty much Italy's best-kept secret. And now I know why. With their majestic mountain peaks, the air so crisp and fresh, and the stunning rocky scenery, it was postcard picturesque. The food was a phenomenal mix of Italian and Austrian delights. People say that the *Selva Val Gardena* is the perfect combination for Italian tourism: The Germanic people run all the ski lifts and manage the city, which keeps everything running smoothly, while the Italians run all the restaurants. I imagine that if they only had this setup for the rest of Italy, it would be the most perfect country in the world.

After a 'white week' or *settimana bianca* as they call it in Italy, my legs were certainly starting to feel the pain. Going off to get a soothing massage, I recollected the last time my legs had felt this sore. Although it didn't come from pleasure, the pain had been delivered as punishment at the hands of my dad. Not the kind of guy to employ 'time outs,' my dad would let us have it at the drop of a hat; my mom totally helpless in front of his frequent firestorms. My offense had been to clear the dinner dishes, unwittingly scooping the potatoes off the plate and into the rubbish bin. My gym teacher took one look at the welts on my legs and sent me straight to the principal's office. He called my mom and told her that he would have to report the incident. My mother came to take me out of school, offering somewhat apologetically, "Well, you see, with eleven children sometimes things get out of hand." But to me, as much as I loved him, it was still my dad who seemed to be the one who was totally out of hand.

Although feeling a bit sore, I was perfectly pleased with myself: not only did I now know where the Dolomites were, but I could also say I had skied upon them. Or rather, I could say that to everyone but my coworkers and my boss. As we came down from the mountain, it was far too soon to leave those white peaks behind us and head back to Rome. Once more we parted ways; this time me going right, Fausto going left. It was clear that at this juncture, we would have to put these forks in the road to an end in short order. Little did I know just how quickly that order might be up.

CHAPTER VIII

~~

Leaving Las Vegas

Summer, fall, then winter with Fausto. Now the challenge was to see it through to the spring. *Fausto's Four Seasons.* Back home in San Diego, although the weather was balmy, I still had the winter blues. Simply put, my days were joyless without my adorable, quirky Italian *amore*. I would put on Bocelli, Pavarotti, Puccini; anything just to *feel* the Italianness wash over me. I felt like the guy in *Breaking Away*—practicing my Italian, watching Italian films, pining away for the pines of Rome. Carlsbad, California, couldn't have been further away. I had finally fallen in love with someone. My life was playing out like the tales of longing and loss of the arias emanating from my stereo. But then again, doesn't someone always die in the end?

For the time being, I had to quit daydreaming and get ready for another tedious investment conference. This time, it would be Las Vegas. How much I used to love the travel, but nowadays

I absolutely dreaded packing my bags and going to yet another airport if I would not be finding Fausto waiting for me on the other side. Upon arrival, instead of those warm, familiar hands around my eyes, I'd be met by someone sticking their hand out to shake mine. I knew I'd have to muster up my best selling face, but the truth was it was all growing far too unbearable to stand much longer. My spirit down in the dumps, I settled in to sit through another mind-numbing conference just so I could sell advertising space to various companies during the breaks; hoteliers, architectural firms, management companies, basically anyone in attendance was a potential target. But these people were no longer a bull's-eye that I wanted to hit. I was bored stiff, demoralized and distressed over my circumstances. If love conquers all, couldn't there be a better way to rout this—and re-route my long-distance relationship?

Out of the blue, strange destiny decided to lend a helping hand. During the opening cocktail reception, I started up a conversation with one of my advertisers from an international architecture studio. He wondered openly how he would get back to his hotel since he had not rented a car. I told him that I had a car and could give him a lift back to the hotel, which turned out to be the same place where I was staying. Naturally, during the drive, we started speaking about his business, the firm's development, his needs, and all those boring conference-type conversations one has in order to fill up the air space with people you hardly know. He then pitched the 64 million dollar question: He asked if I might know anyone that would be interested in a marketing position in his London office. The former marketing executive had just left, and he was thinking about expanding the position to include business development as well. I nearly caused the conversation to end quite abruptly as I stopped straight on a dime; slamming the brakes so hard I nearly sent the guy who could become my future employer right through the dashboard window. I looked over at him and said that, of course, I knew the perfect person for the position... *Me!* He couldn't believe that I would want to up and move away from San Diego, so, I gave him the *Cliff Notes* version of my romance with Fausto. I explained, in no uncertain terms, how much easier it would be for us to see each other if I were based in London. The commute would be just a hop, skip and a two-hour jump by plane, instead of a long-haul 18-hour ride through nine time zones. The idea that this deal of a lifetime—*my lifetime*—could actually come through for me was almost too much to handle. Wielding all my best sales tools I had at my disposal, I took the opportunity to tell him that I would be in London shortly for a hotel equipment show. Perhaps I could stop by his London office to meet the executive team. "It wouldn't cost you anything, and we could move to the next step quickly if it worked out."

My heart absolutely started racing when I heard him say, "Well, why not? Your background is a great fit for this position, and you have just the tenacity we're definitely looking for." That night I could barely shut my eyes tossing about the prospect that fate had brought my way. I could just hear my mother saying that this happenstance, like the one with Fausto at the *Trevi Fountain*, was proof again of another GMC, a God-Manufactured Coincidence. I finally drifted off to sleep with visions of London filling my head... What if?

London Dreams

Another conference, another city. Although this time, instead of being barely able to contain my boredom, I was jittery for what would come ahead. My 'Get out of jail free' card and 'Get closer to Fausto' ticket was just a few hours away. I could not wait to get to my interview with the three managers who made up the Executive Committee of the London office that handled almost all the business across Europe and the Middle East. I was confident it would go well; I was totally qualified, I had both sales and hotel experience plus a business development background, and I knew I would do whatever it took to bring in the business once given the opportunity. I absolutely had to shine. My entire future—and what a lackluster one it would be if I were stuck in San Diego—depended on it.

I arrived at the office to be greeted by a splendidly sweet English woman named Debra, right out of central casting. "Good morning," she said straight away, "You must be Ms. Tondelli—we have been waiting for you." She then offered me tea and biscuits, a perfectly British cordiality that tickles me pink still today. It's a practice that always seems to me so very proper, it never fails to make me feel like royalty. She said that the Managing Director was in a meeting, but would be with me in just a few moments. I sat down, totally thrilled to be right in that chair, in this office, in London, and ready to sign the dotted line with nary a passing thought of what it was that I might be getting myself into.

About 15 minutes later, the Managing Director arrived. Or at least I thought it might be he. This guy walked in with a brusque "Hello" without so much as extending a hand. Incredibly, he was dressed as though he was going to repaint the walls of the office. He was not quite the uppity British Managing Director of an international design firm I had quite envisioned. In fact, he was Scottish and, like his dress, so was his way of speaking English. It was almost impossible to understand a word out of his mouth. That minor detail was of little consequence anyway, because upon greeting me, he curtly followed with the notion that he only had a few minutes to dedicate to our meeting. I had come all the way from San Diego for "a few minutes?" I could tell this was not going to go as swimmingly as I thought it would—or should. Not only was he not as friendly as the charming receptionist, but clearly he did not have time for marketing concepts as well. Trailing him into his office, it was palpable that he was not particularly fond of Americans either, especially one bubbling over with unbridled enthusiasm and ideas. I was starting to feel my foundations quake.

He started off the meeting with a highly encouraging preamble that I strained to understand in more ways than one: "You know, we really don't think we need a marketing person in this office and we certainly don't want someone butting their head in our clients' business." This vote of confidence was quickly followed by, 'The marketing position is Elliott's idea. We want you to know that we are wholly against a marketing person. You know, architects are like doctors; you have to be recommended. You can't have someone going around and selling your services." I was taken so far aback that I lost my faculty for speech. In fact, I had taken such a preemptive hit that I nearly lost all my other faculties as well.

Stammering to my senses, I reminded myself that no company today could rely purely on their merits and relationships. Architecture was a highly competitive field, times were tough, and everyone was trying to drum up more business. I had done some research prior to my meeting and found that almost every architectural office in the marketplace had a business development person on staff. But just as quickly as I had collected my thoughts for a surefire comeback I heard him say he had to go. I could meet another one of the three managers, however, who would be instrumental in making the hiring decision.

Whew. Where was my GMC when I needed it now? I just hoped the next guy would be a bit more receptive to the idea of hiring a marketeer. Much to my chagrin, this first meeting would be a cakewalk compared to the fire walk of the one that followed. I was introduced to John, who, in all his pomposity, did his best to reveal that he was a Senior Partner in the firm. John was an elderly gentleman who probably should have retired a few years earlier. I could tell immediately that he was the classic pensioner whose life had centered around his glorious past. Like his predecessor, he too, was overtly hostile, stating right upfront that he didn't have a lot of time to spend with me. Great. I felt like I had been sent on a fool's errand; told to go sell rancid whale meat to a hostile tribe of Eskimos. He proceeded to quiz me with random questions pulled from a remote part of his anatomy in an attempt to trip up the lame dame American; what with our geographically-challenged reputation. He asked if I knew what the UAE was and if I could name all the countries that comprised it. Adding for good measure and as proof of his Master of the Universe status, that it would be useless to continue the interview if I couldn't regurgitate this most basic knowledge.

"You have got to be kidding," I thought to myself. Ignoring his trick question, I instead made an attempt to sway the conversation in my direction. "Don't you want to review my résumé or discuss what I can bring to your firm?" This absurd notion went nowhere and fast, as I was met with a perfunctory, "No, not really. You know, all of our business is in the Middle East and we really would prefer someone who spoke Arabic." Pausing, to strike just the right note of condescension, he added, "Do you speak Arabic?" Seeing that at this point I had nothing to lose, I shot back that I had many other valuable skills. I thought I could be very helpful in capturing new business, maintaining relationships with current clients and building marketing presentations to consultants, hotel companies, and other key prospects. In short, I could be instrumental in garnering new business from areas they had not yet sought out on a strategic basis. I persisted now with a vengeance, feeling I was regaining my groove. "You can't put all your eggs in one basket, now could you? What if the bottom falls out of the Middle East?" As if I had just delivered my entire value proposition in Chinese, in reply he rose from his chair and said that he had to take another call. Seeing how much I needed it, he then wished me good luck before presenting me to the third manager.

By this time, though, I was filling out my britches. I would see their despondency three-fold. My mom always said I had been born a fighter, and I wasn't going to let a couple of pasty-faced chaps with overblown egos derail my dream to live in Europe and be with Fausto. In the very least, I wouldn't go down without a fight. My twin sister and I had been born quite premature. And although she clocked in at regular weight, I was the lightweight preemie. The nurses informed my mom that she would have to leave me at the hospital and inside an incubator. My mother told them that if that were the case, she'd be more than happy to drop me off and come fetch me in six months' time. In fact, she added, with already eight kids at home—my twin sister making nine—she was inclined to leave me there in their care for good. Needless to say, I came home that very day along with my twin sister, both of us bundled up in my mom's arms.

The fact was, I deigned to grow a bit more optimistic after being told my next interview would be with an American. At least he wouldn't grill me on my knowledge of the Risk game board of continents and emerging countries. They say that the U.S. and the U.K. are two countries divided by a common language. After these first two meetings in these lofty premises, I would say the culture gap was so vast that we were galaxies apart. At long last, I would have a conversation with someone who spoke my same tongue. So far, my business savvy, usual glowing demeanor and sales skills had not served me well.

Although he was one iota more pleasant than the first two, he too, struck a note of uncurbed enthusiasm: *"I'm sorry, but I have very little time."* I thought to myself, "What was Debra the receptionist putting in that tea of hers? Maybe she should lay off the tea altogether and switch over to chamomile." Encouragingly, he did say that even though he felt the need to have a business development and marketing person, in the end, he had very little say in the matter. And although it heartened me to hear that he did not have a great relationship with the other two gentlemen, he also said he really couldn't give me any prospects. Great. The one guy who might have had my back was sitting it out on the bench. Although I refused to show it, I left the office totally dejected. I felt like Charlie Brown having his football pulled right out from under him—yet again.

To say I was disillusioned was an understatement. I was completely crestfallen. I boarded the plane heading for a 14-hour trip back home totally depressed. My dreams of having a small flat in London where I could commute every other weekend to Rome to see the love of my life were fading away as fast as the landscape beneath me. But not one to call it quits at the drop of a hat, once back home I vowed to start conjuring up new escape plans for a way to get myself over to Europe. At least I had a goal to work towards.

I rang Elliott the very next day to discuss my trial by fire at the hands of his cheerful colleagues "across the pond." Concurring my sentiments exactly, he replied meekly, "I didn't want to say anything to you before your interview with them. I knew you would receive less than a warm welcome." Only half-jokingly, I told him in no uncertain terms just how very grateful I was for the surprise ambush. Much to my astonishment, he then continued, telling me that in the end it would be his decision to hire; in any case, he was glad I had the opportunity to meet them. In closing, he said that he would let me know his decision within the week. I couldn't believe

97

my ears. There was still a glimmer of hope that I would make the move to London?

As I hung up the phone, I started weighing out my future prospects. Did I really want to be thrown like an innocent lamb straight into the lion's den? Then again, I supposed if it got me over to London and closer to Fausto, I guess I could bear it. Heck— growing up in a household with ten other siblings…and I was afraid of a few milquetoast Englishmen? I decided I would focus on my goal: Fausto, and go back to daydreaming of charming English pubs and ski vacations in the Alps. One week went by…but one with no news from Elliott. I mustered up my courage and decided that no news would be good news. Two more days, then three…Although I was fast losing faith, still I tried to stay positive, thinking, "Oh well, maybe these guys went to the moon as well." Besides, with the planetary differences between us, convincing them to take me on would make a lunar landing look easy by comparison.

After another week went by with no word from Elliott, I decided to go back to looking at other options. Just then, out of the blue came the call. I picked up the phone to hear Elliott's voice at the other end. He told me that he had decided to hire me despite the opposition of the directors in the London office. With some resignation, he said it really wouldn't matter who he put in that position; they would be against Margaret Thatcher herself. In his gregarious manner, he then asked, "Are you ready to make the move to London?" I hung up the phone, positively dumbfounded. I couldn't decide if I should jump for joy or jump off a long pier. It was the best news ever and I couldn't wait to tell Fausto. Then again, working in a hostile environment would be no easy feat. I could sell anything, but I couldn't even sell myself to Ebenezer Scrooge & Co. Who the heck cared, I would be in Europe!

Next up: arranging my entire exit plan. So much to do, so little time, and no, Sir Elliott, to answer your question, I am decidedly not ready to move to London! I came up with a To Do List: first item on the agenda, quit my job. That would be the easy part. I simply would put in a call to my boss, followed by an email resignation in writing. Second, call my mom. What in the world was I going to tell Mary Lee who had finally settled down in California, just fifteen minutes away from my home? After so many years of living so far apart, I would now be across the Atlantic. And she lived on the Pacific. They may call it 'the pond,' but from San Diego, there was an entire span of country to traverse before you made it to that body of water. What about my sisters, brothers, and support group for so so many years? London was a world away from everyone—everyone, that is, except the guy I had met just over a year before. How time had just flown by. We were going on fifteen months straight of fun, laughter, romance and above all, true friendship and trust. They had been the most wondrous months in four decades of my humble existence. Not even my own mother could come between me and this Golden Opportunity. Next, I needed to find a renter for my house. No sense in putting it on the market—I figured I needed a safety net in case the job didn't work out, or worse—the romance. I had to sell lots of stuff. I was pretty sure I would be moving into a flat about the size of my garage. What to bring with me? I was growing overwhelmed by the thought of it all.

By now seriously in the throes of a massive panic attack, I started going from item to item: What would I do with my car? How could I leave my beautiful house, the one I just spent two years remodeling? What about my friends? Damn time zones! It was too late to call Fausto for moral support. He would always quip, *"I want to be da cozy den for you whenever you're sad about someteeng."* And now, just when I needed the comfort of sanctuary, I'm met with a black hole of time zones instead. I sat myself down in front of the fire with a glass of wine to calm myself down and regain my grip. Taking a few deep breaths and a few deeper sips, I stopped to take a full assessment of what it was I was doing. I was basically about to upend my entire life for a fountain hanger; one that I had practically just met and one with whom I did not even share a common language nor even an area code.

Furthermore, what if it was all just one big, fat lie? I had already been down this path. And not only once, but, counting other live-in relationships, a handful of times before. No matter how far I had come, as far as I was concerned, I was always living in the shadow of my father. These guys sold themselves well, charming their way straight into the arms of trusting, totally naive women. My ex had first claimed to have one child; then I found out there were two. By way of explanation, and not that it made truly a bit of difference in my life, he then said the second was adopted, so he didn't see him as his own. That alibi held water until I saw pictures of a tiny pink baby with his ex-wife in a hospital bed, holding their newborn. He also proclaimed to have a job, a steady income, investments, you name it. He was a certified, pathological liar and I had swallowed his tall tales hook, line and sinker. Every last one of them. More than anything, I just wanted to follow my heart and be in love the storybook way, *Happily Ever After*. People love to quip, *"Watch what you wish for."* My dreamboat had finally come into dock—so why did it feel like a shipwreck?

I called a few girlfriends, who were everything but supportive. Like the guys in the London office, they all seemingly were reading from the same script. One by one, I heard each of them say I must be totally crazy to pack up my house and move to another country for a guy I had only met a year and a few months before, and in front of a fountain, no less. Forgetting how much they had liked him initially, they now rehashed an exhaustive laundry list of caveats for dismantling my entire life for a great guy. In no particular order, their litany of reasons ran along the same philanderer theme; one that I was sadly accustomed to myself: *You know the reputation of Italian men, they're Latin lovers who at first are charming and passionate but then you find out they have two wives, three kids and you are just the pasta-of-the-week...Sooner or later, they'll find another hot dish that they like even better...*I countered with, "He doesn't have another family, I've met his parents, even!" But my protestations only served to boost my own resolve...In the end, I supposed, they were just doing their best girlfriend duty.

Hanging up, I was transported back to my mother's side. We were standing in front of a Chicago pawnshop, her hands over her face while she tried to hide her tears. We were penniless and she had brought me along to sell off her family treasures: rings, jewelry, coats, furs, anything to help her feed the lot of us. My father, the lout, was already with his new wife, thirty years his junior, and making a whole new life—without us. He refused to pay neither child support nor alimony, so my mom had to make ends meet any way she possibly could. Adding insult to injury, she could hardly afford to take off work with no pay to chase down a deadbeat dad. Each time she tried the judge would always say, "I'm sorry, Mrs. Tondelli, there is nothing I can do. Your husband is clearly not working and unable to pay up." Although she was in tears here at the shop, in front of that judge, my mother would always bring out her fightin' Irish side. She would stand up and blurt out, "I know *exactly* where he's working! You can go there yourself and see that he is playing piano at the Golden Palace Restaurant! But he makes sure he's paid in cash so he can get out of paying me!" She would stomp out of the courtroom and then, and only then, would she break down in tears.

While my dad was busy pounding away at the piano keys and—audaciously—making new babies he could barely afford to keep, we were fending for ourselves just across town. We had to leave our nice house in suburbia to move into a tiny apartment in one of the toughest areas of Chicago at the time, an area called Logan Square. It was a far cry from its gentrified glory of urban chic filled with lofts and converted brownstones. Ours was a two-bedroom apartment housing the remaining five of us who were still too young to leave home. It was nicely situated just in front of a crack house doing brisk business day and night. My older brothers and sisters, by now in their twenties, dispersed around the city and working at various odd jobs, would pass onto my mom whatever little they could spare to help her pay for groceries, gas and rent. Life wasn't a bowl of cherries but one thing was for sure, we all had full trust in our indefatigable Mary Lee, our anchor, our breadwinner; as sure in her unbridled love as in her feisty Irish temperament.

That day, I couldn't imagine just how difficult it must have been for my mother to sell what little jewelry she had just to spend the proceeds on basic food staples. Her marriage annulled and her heart in shatters, perhaps she was hesitant to let go of these mementos of happier times. Or perhaps they were a reminder of what a nice life she once had had—or so she thought. Maybe selling them off was just revenge; liberating her fully of his presence. If only banishing all the memories, the heartache and rancor would be as easy as passing jewelry across a countertop and into the hands of a waiting buyer. I was doubly saddened to think that instead of buying herself a freedom ring with her newfound stash, the money had to go instead toward purchasing godawful boxes of rice and the occasional chicken. Regardless, there she was, pawning her diamond engagement ring and a string of cultured pearls that my father had given her in happier times.

She figured that the money would keep us afloat for at least four or five months, giving her strained teacher's salary a bit of a breather. Without a word, the owner of the pawnshop pulled out his magnifying eyeglass to scrutinize the quality of the carat, the size and the workmanship. As if she, herself, were under the jeweler's lens, my mother ruptured the stone silence. "You know, it's a half carat diamond and of very high quality. And these pearls—they're cultured pearls that I have hardly ever worn. My husband bought them at one of the best-known jewelry shops in all of Chicago." The jeweler didn't even look up. Even at fourteen, I could tell he had heard it all before.

At long last, the pawnshop owner raised his head to look squarely at my mother, the round lens still in his eye, his telltale signature of authority in such matters. I heard him say, "I am really sorry to tell you this, lady, but your half carat diamond is only a quarter carat—and your cultured pearls are only costume jewelry. I can't give you much for either one of these, I'm afraid." I couldn't tell if he was angling to make a better deal on something else, or if he was truly sorry for our plight when he added perfunctorily, "Do you have anything else I should see before I close my shop tonight?"

I still can remember the look on my mother's face as clear as yesterday. But to this day, I am unable to discern if the look revealed the shock of finding herself without enough money for her family, or the embarrassment of being 'found out' by a pawnshop guy, or the horror of finally hearing that the love of her life had been a sorry fraud. With a frozen stare across her face, she said softly, "No, nothing more," then turned around, walked out the door, and then sat right down on the steps to cry. True to her strong Irish will, she finally gathered herself together, and without a word, we left for home—the faux jewelry nestled back in her purse. It was at that very moment that I vowed I would never ever find myself in this kind of situation—over any guy. I understood then and there that men would always come to disappoint you.

One big happy family...
(I'm on my big brother's knee)

...And twins make 10

Perhaps my girlfriends were right. Maybe I was too trusting of Fausto. Maybe I was simply an eager buyer and he a shmaltzy salesman. Maybe this whole whirlwind romance meant nothing to him, and I was just one more in a long line of fountain pickups. Once he reached his *Americana* target, he'd lose interest and go sharpshooting for the next one. What had I been thinking? I resolved to go douse my doubts with a few drinks with my girlfriends. Going out the next evening, my girlfriends pulled a stunning 360. They reassured me that after getting to know Fausto, they had truly understood how much he really cared for and loved me. They insisted I was probably doing the right thing, and they'd probably be right there with me if they were in my shoes. Great. Just when I decided to forfeit the race, there I was again, back at the starting line. Once again, I thanked God for good girlfriends when you needed them most. I was beginning to feel just like those astronauts who prepare everything to shoot for the moon, and then, a cloud gets in the way and they have to postpone the flight—indefinitely.

All in all, I came to the conclusion that I really had nothing to lose. I would still have my house, my friends, my family to come back to in case it didn't work out. Inside, I felt that I just had to do this, no matter what the risks. My mind was made up. I wouldn't be able to live with myself if I'd blown the chance of a lifetime for true blue love. Seeing that everything in my life seemed to revolve around six-week intervals, so it was with London. I would be leaving to work for *Scrooge and Marley & Co.* in just six weeks' time.

Thelma & Louise

Finally at peace with myself, my situation and my heartfelt decision, I gathered up my soft and lovely Thelma to cuddle on my lap when my heart stopped—*completely*. What in God's name would I do about my babies, Thelma & Louise? England had a vicious quarantine law. I had heard that they lock up animals in cages for six full months upon arrival at their supposed pristine island. This was a cruel card to deal anyone, let alone these two innocent creatures. I was quite certain that they would never survive a horrendous confinement like that. My cats, like most helpless animals, required tons of love and attention. How could I abandon them to their fate at the hands of pasty-faced prison guards?

With the last of the boring investment conferences well behind me, I flew to London to look for an apartment, get my working papers in order, and process all of the necessary hiring documents to start my new life in the architect studio of Ebenezer Scrooge himself, had he been alive at the turn of the 21st century. But he and his partners were the least of my problems. I had a much more worthy nemesis to worry about: the quarantine officer in charge of animal imports whose very presence left me quaking in my boots. He reiterated what I already knew: Thelma & Louise would be incarcerated in a pint-sized cage—potentially surrounded by herds of sick animals—for the better part of six cruel, cuddle-free months. It was like hearing the death knell being rung by Cruella de Vil herself.

Thelma & Louise

106

After forcing the quarantine warden into lengthy negotiations reminiscent of the Palestinian peace talks, he finally submitted a terrific compromise: "Well, there is one way around this, you see. You can have someone in Europe keep them for six months rather than have them kept in quarantine here." And while they would still need to have their microchips, vaccines, and all the necessary shots before coming to Europe, that was a petty inconvenience compared with a life behind bars. Of course, there was one stumbling block: Fausto, the only European I knew, was the furthest thing from Tarzan of the Jungle I could ever summon to take on this enterprise. In fact, he was pretty much the last person on Earth I envisioned taking care of my cats; precisely the same sentiment he expressed summarily to me on the phone that very evening. The babies, much like their human counterparts, would prove to be the greatest challenge of our intercontinental relationship. In fact, it's fairly safe to say that animals are probably the bane of cross-cultural existence for any couple—worldwide. What happened when those pilgrims set foot in the New World, I wondered, to have brought such a divergence of opinion when it came to domestic animals? I decided to just put it to him straight. "Okay, my darling, here is the deal...I have found a way to come to London to be closer to you and we can see each other every weekend. But all this comes with just one hitch: You need to take the babies for six months. Just six. They will have to live with you until I can bring them into England." The phone went dead.

"Fausto, are you there?" This was the final hurdle. I held my breath. Until finally, *"Well, you know, my love, I am not so good manager of da babies...I mean, I never had a cat before and I don't know if I can be a good manager of dem. You know, it ees a big reesponsa'bileety...Can we discuss eet tomoarrow?"* "Tomorrow??! Why tomorrow? No, I need an answer right now." *"But you know my love, my apartment isa notah so beeg and where do I put the toilet for them?"* This time, it was me who took a pregnant pause. I mean, I have uprooted my entire existence, changing jobs, houses, and country, and he's worried about the litter box? In the end, he finally thought better of it and gave in. *"Okay, I weell manage*

107

them, but you have to teach me how to manage them okay? You see, Italians have a much deefferent relationship with their animals than Americans...I mean, most of our cats here in Roma leeve outside, do you understand, my love?" I heaved a huge sigh of relief. Later, he would confess that his mother was absolutely mortified to learn that my cats would be occupying the same quarters as he. In retrospect, it was tantamount to an American being asked to take in a squirrel or a wild opossum to live as a pet. Believe me, Italians may have cornered the market on civilization, but in terms of what they think of animals, they are still in the Dark Ages. No wonder they never warmed up to Cleopatra. She kept ghastly snakes for pets.

No matter, this one last bullet had been dodged effectively. I was on my way to London via Rome, to leave my beautiful babies behind and in the care of pernickety Fausto. Little did I know that that would be the easy part. My girls needed one last check-up before departure, and I needed one last meeting with my veterinarian to make sure that all the documentation was in order. Shots, forms, histories for two; all translated into Italian so I could pass customs with flying colors and settle the cats onto foreign soil. I prayed that meant sand from an Italian litter box, and not Roman dirt after Fausto had let them loose in the Forum. I had read the regulations online that the Italian authorities would be checking every detail upon arrival at Rome's airport. All in all, it made some sense: you can't very well bring in as much as a piece of *parmigiano* into the USA, I could just imagine importing two live animals into Italy.

At the San Diego airport, I finally heard the last boarding call for the flight to New York. My mom and my twin sister had come to see me off. My nephew, Leo, only two at the time, started screaming his head off as I started down the ramp to board the plane with my two kitties. "Don't go, Hotsy!! Don't go!!!" shouted Leo after me. 'Hotsy' was the nickname given to me by my twin sister when we were about two, because she couldn't pronounce my name, Cathy. How strange it was to be called that by a fresh generation of Tondelli's. How much we had grown up. On hearing his outburst, I chuckled all the way onto the plane—I'm sure more than a few eyebrows were raised amongst the passengers as I turned to walk down the gangway and onto my new life abroad. My mom, giving me one last lookover before departure repeated what she had said the very day I came home from Rome after my first test drive with Fausto: "I've lost my baby to Rome." I waved goodbye as well as I could while carrying two kitties and a six-month supply of all of my earthly possessions. In fact, I only needed to get through the next six months. I had taken out a six-month lease on a flat that I absolutely despised but that was close to the office. That would give me time to get my bearings, check out the neighborhoods and the commute before settling down to a place I could call 'home.' One look over my shoulder and I knew there was no turning back now. Off we were on our five-hour flight to New York and then another nine hours onto Rome; me, with Thelma & Louise stuffed under my seat. I said a quiet prayer that everything would go smoothly.

In New York City, we were informed that my connecting flight to Rome had been delayed to 12:00 pm—the following day. I was absolutely dumbfounded. Overladen with my furry bundles and everything else besides, I begged the agent, "You have got to be kidding. I have two cats, two huge suitcases, and *now* what do I do for the next 18 hours?" Her remarkable response? "You will have to sleep at a hotel near the airport and come back tomorrow. There is nothing I can do about it." My massive life upheaval seriously was not getting off to a good start. Was this a sign that I should turn around and go back home? Was this yet another date with destiny messing with my future? It seemed for every two steps forward, I always managed to take one step back. Down but not out, off the three of us went to check into the nearest hotel to JFK Airport. I checked into the room only to discover that, naturally, a five-pound bag of kitty litter wasn't one of my carry-on items. I placed them in the bathtub and hoped for the best. Out of their environment and scared from all the coming and goings on, they slept under my bed until daybreak. Back in the cage and nine more hours in flight, we would finally reach their new home in Rome.

At Rome arrivals, I approached the customs counter, wielding all my documents like a drum major rushing into the stadium and onto the field. I was totally prepared for animal control. Suddenly, one of the Italian officials took one look at my cats and exclaimed in Italian, "*Ma guarda che carini! Che razze sono?—Just look how cute they are! What kind of cats are they?*" Taken by surprise, I told him they were Siamese. He smiled and looked fondly at Thelma & Louise, who, after over eleven hours stuffed in a cage at 30,000 feet were decidedly less than receptive to this odd welcoming committee. Seeing that the conversation wasn't heading anywhere near more official banter, I ventured to steer the officer back to his duty. With some trepidation, I offered up by matter of course, "Don't you need to see my cats' documents?" Still caressing my kitties, he answered, "No, we don't need to see anything. You can go ahead, *Signora. Benvenute a Roma!*" I couldn't believe my ears. *Che bella, Italia!* Now, if only Fausto's reception would be this buoyant.

CHAPTER IX

❧

An American Lone Wolf in London

My first few weeks at my new office in London were positively torturous, a term I picked up from Fausto ("*una tortura*," or 'torture' as Fausto would exclaim periodically about anything he didn't like to do) and which most accurately characterized my situation. I liked to think of it as some sort of trial by fire; thankfully one that only made weekends with Fausto so much more refreshing and revitalizing. Each morning, I would be greeted with a smile by Debra, the picture perfect English receptionist straight out of central casting. Just like on the day of my interview, she'd offer me a nice English tea, rain or shine. Unfortunately, heading into a UK winter, it was more rain than shine. Even more unfortunate was the knowledge that this nicety would be the highlight of my entire day. As I walked into my office, things would slide quickly downhill from there. The atmosphere around the office could not have been more noxious. I was treated more like a leper than an asset for the future growth of the firm. As the days ground on, I began to think that Debra didn't offer me a tea out of pure courtesy; it was more likely out of sheer pity. She would cast me a knowing look while watching me day in, day out trying to break through to the three partners who evidently had decided to pretend that I simply did not exist. Debra would become not only my only office ally but also eventually one of my best friends. She was a virtual lifesaver for me, the cast-away in London; printing out maps of wherever I needed to go, telling me which tube (subway) stop I needed to get off at; in short, unabashedly acting more like my surrogate mother than my coworker.

Almost daily I would be overcome with pangs of anxiety, generally peppered with self-doubt and a rather healthy dose of revenge. When not feeling dejected, I'd prod myself thinking, "Why do I have to prove that I can win these guys over when I could be basking in the sun in *Piazza Navona* licking a large scoop of creamy pistachio *gelato*?!" Fortunately for me, I'd inherited my mom's tenacious Irish spirit, and I steadfastly refused to cave to their silent treatment. My very own father cut me off for over 20 years and I not only survived, I thrived in his absence. Certainly, I could get through a day at the office. By now, it had become a test of wills. Regrettably, on most days I still felt I was flunking the test. Just weeks into what was supposed to be my exciting London adventure, I found myself totally shut out: isolated and alone by day, lonesome in a hideous apartment by night, which is exactly what they wanted.

Lassie Come Home

Returning at night to my depressing one-room flat—*"the mouse cave,"* as Fausto had charmingly christened it—felt like entering a prison cell. Ignored by my jailors by day, in solitary confinement by night...It seemed as though I were reliving the worst episode in my life when, against my will, I was forced to move in with my father. My *Year of Living Depressingly* occurred not long after my dad had left us and started a new life with his new wife. It began on account of a dog that happened to look like Lassie. She had been a gift from one of my dad's band members, perhaps as a token indulgence to get our minds off of losing our dad. Certainly we could forgive him through the presence of this beautiful fluffy dog in his stead. She turned out to be just as problematic to have around as my dad had been. And although the dog had all kinds of behavioral issues, my twin sister, Christine, wanted to keep her at all cost. Little did I know how high the price tag would be for her compassion. The Lassie dog had already sent Christine to the hospital three times, and now, for the love of this insane dog, we'd both be sent straight to the asylum. My mom had taken one look at the dog and immediately declared that there would be no way we could afford to keep her. Trying to squeeze money for dog food out of our measly budget was like trying to get blood from a turnip, my Irish grandmother would say. As it stood, we were already living off the rejected candy I would bring home from my job at Fannie May, along with leftover pies taken at the end of the night shift from my twin's job at Baker's Square. My mother said the only way we could keep the dog was if we had another sibling working the night shift at PetSmart. It was settled, the dog had to go.

Shortly thereafter, we had missed our bus for school, and my mom ended up having to drive us. During the short ride over, my twin told our mom how she had been talking to dad, and that she knew all about the money mom had salted away in Swiss bank accounts. Making matters worse, Christine prattled on about how our poor father was struggling to make ends meet, while my mother had thousands stashed away overseas. Driving the point home, in the way that only a teen knows best, she then conveyed that our dad and his new wife would be *overjoyed* at having us—and, we could take the dog to live with them to boot. I could just see the steam spurting out of my mother's ears. I hadn't seen her this angry since my brother had broken her Madonna statue into a thousand pieces. Of course, it was all nothing but more of my dad's hurtful lies, with my sister parroting them right down to the letter. Without a word, Mary Lee decided she had heard enough. She turned the car around on a dime and hastily drove back to our house. She ran into our room and hurriedly filled two large Hefty garbage bags with as many clothes out of our closet as she could grab in her frantic rage. We didn't know what was going on. She barked at us to get back in the car, and with a swift swoop, she launched the stuffed bags into her trunk with the finesse of the Grinch tossing the gifts back *up* the chimney. The dog had much the same reaction as that of the Grinch's as she was unceremoniously coerced into the car along with our bags. Mary Lee sped over to my grandmother's house, where my father and his new wife were now living in the lap of luxury, and dropped the three of us off right on the doorstep. As my mom pulled away as if leaving the scene of a bank heist, I began to feel sick to my stomach. I took one look at my sister and said, "Now look at the fine mess you've gotten us into. *Now* what do we do?"

Ringing the bell, Christine said it would all turn out just fine; dad really *did* want us there and so did his new wife. At that moment, we saw her peer through the glass panel in the door; it would be the first time I would set sight on the face of the woman who had broken up our family. She was about 30 years old and a born again Christian. One look at the two of us standing there, black plastic garbage bags and a dog in hand, and a look of horror shot across her face. Without even opening the door a crack, nor so much as letting out a peep, she turned straight away as if she had faced down two burglars lying in wait. We stood there, immobile, wondering what she would do next. After an interminable amount of time, she finally opened the door and told us we could come in. She said she had spoken to our dad who said we could stay there for the time being, but that we would need to have a household meeting that evening when he came home. I could tell from that moment on that she had already cast herself in the role of the evil stepmother; determined to make it as difficult as she could for us to feel 'at home' in her tidy love nest. Holed up in my tiny London flat, I struggled to put these thoughts and my emotions at bay. Regardless, I couldn't help but drown myself in my very own misery; except this time, my situation was all my own doing and it wasn't on account of a mangy mutt.

Debra and my other English pal in the office, Diane, my *Charlie's Angels* as I liked to call them, took it upon themselves to humor me and make me feel most welcomed. They could tell I was growing more and more frustrated by the day…If only I could just feel needed at work and contribute something, anything to the office, I would somehow crawl my way out of this depression. I knew I had always been an asset to any company I'd worked for, and my job was truly an integral part of my identity and a great source of pride. Flung out of my comfort zone and far from my country, it seemed that everything was contrived against me. Even my real boss, Elliott, was thousands of miles away, happily ensconced in our Hawaii office. And even when he wasn't in the office, he was travelling all across the map like a modern-day Lewis or Clark, so I couldn't even count on his vote of confidence. As far as Elliott was concerned, I was out of sight and out of mind. Down on the count, I took a deep breath, got up and back into the ring, determined not to throw in the towel.

One day, Debra and Diane told me that they had a surprise to cheer me up. They had bought tickets to the musical, *Mamma Mia!* playing in London's West End. It was a really sensational show and the three of us had a fun-filled evening out on the town; so much so, that even my spirits were lifted, at least for one evening. That night, while saying my prayers, I decided to put in a special request to Saint Anthony. "Dear St Anthony, please help me find a way to win over these men who don't want me here. Please help me find happiness working in this insanely difficult environment." Right on cue, the telephone rang. It was a distress call from my mom. She phoned to tell me that her sister had passed away. I was surprised to hear my mom so upset about losing her sister since they hadn't been on the best of terms in their later years. This was a bad omen if I had ever seen one.

My mother and my aunt were polar opposites. Whereas my mom had legions-deep of warmth and kindness reserves, my aunt was ice cold and very rigid. Whereas my mom had held out for her one true love and stuck by her man through thick and thin, my aunt was a tawdry version of Elizabeth Taylor: ultimately marrying seven times, twice to the same man. It was hard to fathom how so many guys could fall for this distant and disdainful woman, and not for her sweet, pretty and smart sister. Although my aunt had been quite a looker back in her day, the older they grew, it was my mother who turned out to possess the real beauty, both inside and out. Speaking of sisterhood, in closing, my mom brought up how concerned she was about my twin sister, Christine. Christine's husband recently had accepted a job transfer, and she found herself back in Chicago and slowly sinking into a severe depression. She had left behind the sun, friends, and a lovely ranch home in Phoenix that she had just finished renovating, for the brutally cold winters and unbearable summers of *The Windy City*. Listening to her voice her concerns, I couldn't bring myself to tell my mom, that I, too, was totally down and out and that I could barely muster the energy to head into the office each day. Before hanging up, she asked, "Honey, could you just give your twin sister a call to cheer her up?" I told her I would as soon as we were off the phone. But drained from the emotional rollercoaster of the evening, I fell into a deep sleep instead. I awoke with a start in the middle of the night with a terrifying nightmare. I dreamt that my twin sister was having a heart attack. Breaking into a sweat, I just knew in my heart that she was in serious trouble. I phoned her immediately to find her lying on a gurney in the emergency room—thinking she was having a heart attack.

It's said that twins seem to share an inherent knowledge of their twin's emotional state. The two of us had had telepathic experiences all of our lives. I could usually detect when something was amiss, or when she was in the throes of a crisis. She had come to mind a great deal the few days prior, so it didn't surprise me to learn that she was also going through a similar depression as mine. I recalled lying on the operating table at twelve just about to have my appendix surgery, when Christine was also rushed into the emergency room. She had suddenly been afflicted with the identical piercing pain in her side. But after a thorough checkup she was released, the doctor telling my parents that it was merely a case of 'sympathy pain' for me. So here we were, both going through a state of depression together due to our life trajectories. But this time, it was my turn to be the strong one to help the two of us through the fog. I tried my best to give her some encouragement before finally putting down the phone and falling fast asleep.

Hours later, I awoke to a stream of sunshine beaming through my bedroom window. This was the first ray of sunshine after an eternity of cold, rainy, grey weather. I took it as another sign from God that helped bolster my spirits. Feeling uplifted, I took extra care getting ready that morning deciding to wear my favorite beige Max Mara suit; one that Fausto had bought me for my birthday back in August. Putting it on, I could practically hear my mom by my side chirping, "If you look good, you feel good and if you feel good, you do good." Of course, she was right. I felt good that morning. On the way to the office, I told myself that this was the day I was going to break them. I began to psych myself out like a tennis player readying for Wimbledon. I was not going to let these three stooges ruin the chance of a lifetime. By the time I reached the office door, I was determined to invite the head of the office to lunch. Stepping across the threshold, I could tell that perhaps St Anthony had found me the peace I so desired.

After my morning ritual over tea and biscuits with Debra and Diane, I screwed up the courage to head up to the third floor and into the General Manager's office. Like an unwanted guest, I had been relegated to a first floor office in the interior design department, in order to keep me well out of sight and easily out of mind. Taking a deep breath, I walked briskly into Tom's office to ask him if he was free for lunch. Upon seeing me, he threw a preemptive strike that caught me totally off guard. "Hey, are you available for lunch today?" he said in a tone that I was positive was approaching one iota of warmth; like when those early rays on a subzero day cause the icicles to drip. "Wow!" I thought, "These GMC coincidences are certainly tailor-made!" I replied that in actual fact I was free and would be delighted to join him for lunch. I let him know that I had prepared a set of strategic marketing objectives I had in mind for the business and wanted to review them with him. And for the second time in about as many minutes, he blindsided me once again. "Oh, no, Catherine, I can't make it today. In fact, I have to finish a few drawings for a client in Oman. But I need you to accompany one of our important clients who will be coming in today. We're set to go over the architectural changes on a Greek villa we're designing for him." I was struck dumb. Chatty Cathy, my household name after the 1960s doll that would talk away whenever you pulled a cord on her back, had lost her faculty for speech. Making sure I had heard him correctly and double-checking that my brain synapses were firing properly, I managed to mumble that I would be happy to take his client to lunch. Staring this gift horse straight back down into his tonsils, I added a bold postscript; putting Tom on warning that I did not upheave myself 6,000 miles away from home to take his clients out to lunch. I asked him when we could schedule a lunch to discuss my new role and review my next steps in order to increase his business. He offered his usual milquetoast, "Maybe next week—but for now I need you to help me out." Deciding it was probably best to grab the bone I was being thrown, I said I'd be delighted.

Saint Anthony clearly pulling out all the stops, I couldn't believe it when Tom invited me into the meeting when the client appeared at our offices. It was the first business-related anything I had been party to, and I silently rejoiced in this one small victory. Tom introduced me to an elderly, clearly moneyed man, Michael. Michael seemed so old that I was surprised to hear him so passionately making plans to complete his villa to his liking. It would be the first of many meetings I eventually would have with the international upper crust in order to discuss their architectural follies. Just listening in to the conversation would help me tremendously in future business calls. Tom didn't realize it, but employing me as a decoy would work in my favor in the end. I kept my mouth shut throughout the meeting in order to take it all in, one sickeningly sweet spoonful at a time. I felt like a mole at the CIA. At the end of the meeting, Tom apologized to the client for not being able to join him for lunch, adding coyly that he was a lucky man to have me as his lunch partner. "Great," I thought as Michael accompanied me out of the office, "now I'm a professional escort." I knew Tom was using me as 'eye candy' but as we made our way down to street level, I decided to thank God for opening this one minute window of opportunity. I knew full well that it was a GMC moment that may just turn the tide in my direction.

The Prince of Egypt

Michael and I stepped into his silver blue Bentley he had waiting right outside our office, and I was introduced to his driver, Harry. As we made our way, I could tell that he had not clued into the fact that I knew next to nothing about his project. Finding a new audience in me, he kick-started his laundry list of the few but necessary changes he wanted to make on his seaside villa. The kitchen needed to be larger, as he liked throwing huge parties and the swimming pool needed to be moved to the other side of the house so his guests could watch the sun set on the Aegean Sea. And most importantly, he wanted all of the works completed before he was to wed his second wife, adding with a touch of bragging rights, who happened to be 21 years old. I let out an audible gasp. Michael had to be 80 years old at least. He seemed so old and frail I wondered if he would even live to actually see the sun set over the island of Skopelos by next week.

Michael asked if I liked the dining room at Harrod's as he had a friend who might be joining us. As cool as I could, I said it would be lovely. The truth was, I had been there only once before, twenty years earlier when my mom and I came to visit my little brother, Reno, during his year abroad. I smiled to myself thinking about how, after purchasing our plane tickets, we barely had enough money to pay for our two afternoon teas at Harrod's. My daydream was interrupted by Michael regaling me with tales of his rocky romance. Turns out, the 21-year old girlfriend was not much of a gold digger after all; she plain and simply didn't want to marry him. Her mother, clearly a hopeless romantic, was trying her utmost best to convince her daughter that he would make the ideal husband. Listening to his tale of woe, I could only thank my lucky stars for being graced with the mother I had; Mary Lee would be positively appalled if any of us had so much as murmured that we fancied marrying someone sixty years our senior, at any age. Visions of Anna Nicole Smith and Elliott Marshall rolled through my head. Once seated at a private table, Michael ordered wine with a plate of smoked salmon and caviar to accompany it. Sitting there with what would be the first in a long line of luncheon invitations, I ordered the Dover sole. Well, what a difference seventeen years could make. Then again, they were nothing when compared with the six decades separating this octogenarian and his bride-to-be.

Michael informed me that his friend, Mohamed, had another lunch engagement but would be joining us for dessert. I was relieved to know that someone else might play interference in our charming tête à tête; it was tedious listening to a grown man pout over his baby girlfriend. At long last, we were greeted with a warm, "Good afternoon" and I looked up to see a dark and utterly dashing man at our table. Michael introduced me to him as Mohamed and I held out my hand as I had done so many times before for a handshake. He took it, turned it ever so slightly and gallantly held it up to pursed lips to feign a kiss on the back of my hand, all in one smooth gesture. As he gave me a slight bow with his head, I realized that my hand was in that of Mohamed Al Fayed, the father of Dodi and proprietor of the Hotel Ritz in Paris—and, of course, Harrod's department store. Suddenly, lunch became a whole heckuva lot more interesting. Rehashing the day's events, I had to admit that St Anthony really could pull through in a pinch. And across denominations to boot! Turning on the charm, after only a few moments he told us that he had been thinking about putting Harrod's up for sale. He explained that the royal family had stopped frequenting his store after his son and Princess Diana were killed in that horrible accident in Paris. They even had asked to have the royal crest taken down from its historic berth on the façade. It was common knowledge that Mohamed had been totally outspoken over his theory that the car crash had been the concerted result of a conspiracy against him and his family. Furthermore, he had come to the barefaced conclusion that the entire incident had been magnificently orchestrated by the British royal family itself. It had been a plot to get rid of Diana, he declared, seeing she was dating a Muslim. It would be thirteen years after the death of his son, Dodi, and Lady Di before Mohamed Al Fayed would sell Harrod's for 1.5 billion pounds to the Qatar royal family. Definitively out of British hands, the royal crest has since been removed, just as Mohamed had suggested during our brief meeting.

This highly memorable encounter would be the first of countless luncheons, dinner engagements, black tie parties, and jet setting that I would participate in for my new company. Eventually I would find myself in the loop on more than just royal dirt and I would relish every moment of it. And while I grew accustomed to my new, glitzy fast-paced lifestyle, around the office things would still keep at a snail's pace. It would be weeks before Tom finally took the time to meet with me again and review my plans. Regardless of my business savvy and bright ideas put forth and acted upon, I would still hold the status of *persona non grata*. To make matters worse, the British winter was settling in and the fabled cold, damp, dismal, darkness of London had arrived.

Winter of 2000 would prove to be the wettest winter on record in 100 years. I fell severely ill three times and it wasn't from eating unwashed lettuce in developing countries. It didn't help that for Fausto, each time it was a near-death experience and I needed to get out of that bloodthirsty town as fast as I had come. The first time I called in sick, I mentioned to Debra that the fact that the heating had gone out in my apartment wasn't helping to speed my recovery. Debra came by that very evening with a container of homemade chicken soup and an electric blanket. She was my guardian angel sent down from the heavens; I truly did not know what I would have done without her. We joked that I must have contracted foot-and-mouth or mad cow disease; never had I been so sick so often in such a short span of time.

With Debra nursing me back to health in the evenings, my days were spent staring at the peeling paint on the ceiling. Eventually, I would trudge back into work; it was actually an improvement on my dismal apartment. In the panoply of habitats in my lifetime, my London mouse cave was even worse than my first dismal apartment that I shared with 2 other girls. I hated everything in the flat from the white Formica Ikea wardrobe closet—a white elephant trapped inside a mouse hole—to the awkward bed stuck right in the middle of the flat. Only a contortionist could get their clothes out of the immense closet each morning. Luckily, I had only brought one suitcase full of clothes so I didn't need to use the closet at all. At this rate, I really wasn't sure how long I would last. In the very least, I was grateful for my upbringing of sharing a room with three or more siblings—Who knew our cramped quarters would come in handy one day? All in all, it was the farthest thing from the charming, fashionable London lifestyle I had envisioned. And the worst part yet, I still had months to go before I would have Thelma & Louise on my lap to comfort me when the going got rough; if it could get any rougher, that is.

My mom would phone once a week and tell me how proud she was that I was living in London and working for such a prestigious design firm, with such a privileged position. She told me that she had had the opportunity to move to Paris after college with some girlfriends, but had decided to marry my father instead. It would be 50 years before she would visit Paris, when my sisters and I surprised her with a trip for her 70th birthday. I could tell that she was living out her European dream vicariously through me and the last thing I wanted was to disappoint her by the complexities of my office experience. She would always leave me with one of her sage 'mommisms.' This time it was, *Life is like a roll of toilet paper—the closer you get to the end, the faster it goes. So, make the most of it.* I promised her, I would.

The Towering Inferno

Like those of the preceding generation who remember precisely where they were the day John F. Kennedy was shot in Dallas, all of us who stood testimony to the day's events of September 11th 2001 would recall every minute detail of the day in which "the world would never be the same." On that particular day, I was in London and had just finished lunch with one of the American architects who had come over to work on a project in our office. Walking back into our office, Debra informed me that a terrible tragedy had happened in America: a plane had accidentally crashed into one of the Twin Towers in New York City. She told me they had switched on the TV in the conference room, and I should go in immediately and see the coverage. Walking into the room, I was stunned silent by the horrific images of the aftermath of the plane crash high up in the tower. Holding my breath while holding back tears for those who had died in the crash, I knew it was the beginning of the workday in New York City. How many had also perished while innocently sitting at their desks? Even the newscasters were unable to interpret the harrowing scene that was unfolding in real time. I looked around at the people sitting around the conference room. Their reaction to the events on the screen was playing out as if it were nothing but a cheap B-rated disaster flick.

The room was totally abuzz—managers, designers, architects, secretaries, all intent on carrying out the day's activities: designing hotel rooms, sending plans, chit-chatting about future projects, setting up client meetings. I scanned this beehive of activity, all the more incredulous due to the fact that our office was a mini-United Nations filled with Australians, South Africans, Arabs, Scots, Irish, Finns, you name it. Only a handful of us stood there, immobile, hovering around the television set in utter shock at the billowing cloud of smoke emanating from the tower. As we stood there in disbelief, we heard the BBC newscaster say that a second plane had hit the second tower. Suddenly, the image of the second airplane smashing into the second tower was up on my screen. It was so surreal, it seemed we were tuned into the world at war. I had a sick feeling in my stomach but grew sicker looking around the space to see the others working away at their desks as though it was just another day in New York. Had we become so totally immune to major catastrophes even those unraveling right in our midst?

Shaken, I decided to head back into my office to call my American girlfriend Jan who was also living in London. But before I could dial, my phone rang. It was one of our Palestinian clients for whom we were designing a palace. I was listening to her speak without really hearing the words when suddenly, she asked me if I was American. "Well, yes," I replied, half-expectantly waiting for her to say how awful she felt about what had happened this morning and how sorry she was for my country. Like a shot, she blurted out, "Well, you Americans had this coming! After all the countries you've destroyed, ruined and bombed, this is what you get and you deserve it!" As if this onslaught wasn't enough, and within only an hour of the attacks, she pressed on. Smoke was still billowing out of the towers, and here she was, emphatically spewing the conspiracy theories that would forever shadow this tragic day. She told me that the attack on the Twin Towers was nothing but a plot by the Jews who wanted to get America mad enough to start a war in the Middle East. "You know, those planes were provided for and organized by the Israelis—even the pilots flying them were Israelis." Hearing all of these accusations and from an important client no less, left me clearly at a loss for words. I haltingly spat out the best response I could manage. In so many words, I told her that while I agreed that my country undoubtedly had made mistakes, there was no excuse to treat all Americans alike. I then told her I had to go, but that certainly someone would be contacting her shortly to follow up on the palace she wanted to have built.

With news of the Pentagon attack coming in, and now distraught so far from home or Fausto, I called my mom. She stated in no uncertain terms to lie low as an American overseas—anyone could be a target—and to not do anything or wear anything that might tip someone off that I was from the United States. No one at this point knew where the attacks had come from, nor where they would lead, and here in London, I was all alone. By this time, the towers had collapsed, taking thousands of innocent lives with them. Even newscasters were left speechless by the spectacle and the enormity of the brazen attacks. Around me, people were still busily going about their business as a colony of worker ants. I took a deep breath and tried to make some sense of what had happened and what was going on around me. Feeling terribly lonely and downright grief-stricken, I decided to ignore my mom's advice and join with other Americans who were probably feeling much the same way. Foolishly, I headed over to the United States Embassy, which happened to be located just a few blocks from my office. By this time it was evening in London. I arrived to find a circle of Americans holding hands, others cupping candles, and still others posting photos of loved ones lost in the tragedy. It was a beautiful, heartfelt sight and joining them, I felt somewhat at peace and soothingly connected in some way with my fellow countrymen. We would break into songs of *God Bless America* and *America the Beautiful*. A *USA Today* photographer who had descended upon the scene snapped a photo of me weeping uncontrollably.

Needless to say, this photo ended up being the 'picture worth a thousand words' for media outlets worldwide, trying to capture the zeitgeist of those Americans abroad. The photo seen 'round the world ended up not only in the *London Times*, the *Kuwait Times*, on *CNN*, across internet sites, but even in all my hometown newspapers—my hometown being Chicago, one of the largest media cities in the USA. Friends and family members were phoning from across the country saying they had seen a picture of me crying in front of the US Embassy in London. My mother, who had already been nervous about my living abroad, was now totally beside herself. She envisioned innocents taken down right in the streets, the likes of which you can see in a remake of *War of the Worlds*.

ACTS OF WAR
'USA WILL WIN'

•Five Arabs identified as suspects
•One plane headed for White House
•Toll rising in NY, 800 at Pentagon

LONDON: Cathy Tendell wipes away a tear as she looks at the floral tributes outside the United States Embassy yesterday. — AP photo

Back at the embassy, and only after about fifteen minutes into our spontaneous and peaceful vigil, we were disrupted by a Palestinian woman. She started screaming at us with impudence, drilling us on who was crying for all the Palestinian children killed by Americans with weapons provided to Israel. Hearing her angry words, it dawned on me just how sheltered a life I had been living in America all these years. September 11th 2001 brought a 'coming of age' moment in which I had to respect that I was living in a much bigger world now. I told her I fully understood her pain, but that there was a time and place for everything. Trying to reason with her, I offered that perhaps we should respect the losses for which she, herself had witnessed in her land, but also show respect for the many people gathered here who had also just lost loved ones. From that moment on, it was clear that, for at least one person, the tidy world in which I lived would never ever be the same again.

By nightfall, I was feeling a little bit more tranquil and somewhat relieved to be a lot more connected to the world at large. But the lull in my grief was momentarily eclipsed by an even more immediate dilemma: Fausto and I were scheduled to leave for a ten day trip to Morocco and my flight was leaving at 9 am the very next morning. Seeing what had just transpired in New York City, the last thing I wanted to do was board a plane bound for a Muslim country. I needed to get home and talk to Fausto—and fast.

Leaving the embassy, I discovered the London subways shut down as a preventative measure against further attacks. Buses were running irregularly, if at all. The entire city had taken on an intense and eerie calm, as if we were under a curfew; though this one was self-imposed with most everyone glued to television screens. I ended up having to walk all the way back to my lonely apartment. The walk took me over an hour and along the way, I would peer through pub windows at the Londoners intent on watching news updates as if they were World Cup matches. With each pace, I grew more and more insecure. At home at last, I phoned Fausto right away. Blurting out that I was absolutely unsure I wanted to leave the next morning, Fausto responded in his usual iconoclastic manner: "*Well, I teenk it will actually be one of the most secure days to travel. But, eet ees up to you...I let you decide...*" He was loads of help. I said I would think on it and phone him back in an hour. An hour later, I heard myself saying that I would brave the risks of flying to a Muslim country and go ahead with our plans. At 8:30 am the very next day, I boarded my flight from London to Casablanca. I wouldn't dare breathe a word of this to Mary Lee until I was back safely in London. I may be surrounded by Moroccans, but at least I wouldn't have to field any more Palestinian outrage over geopolitics and its repercussions. So much for wishful thinking.

Road to Morocco

Arriving at the airport, it looked like the curfew was still in force. Planes to the U.S. had been entirely cancelled, and I was taken aback to discover only four other people on my flight. The entire way down, I kept reminding myself of Fausto's words. Of course, Fausto was right. I felt safer than I ever thought I would have been under any other circumstance. Landing at the Casablanca airport, Fausto was there to meet me—never had I been so happy to see him. We hugged each other with all our might. We decided to lie low this first day at our hotel before heading out for dinner. Arriving at a fairly popular restaurant, we found it completely empty of clients. Wondering whether we had happened there in the middle of Ramadan, or worse, if something had happened in Morocco that we didn't know about, we asked the staff about it. Our waiter assured us that it was just a very slow night seeing that many people had cancelled their trips due to the Twin Tower attacks. Although we had the place to ourselves, I, for one, couldn't decide if this was a good thing or something totally creepy. We tried to pay no attention to the fact that we stuck out like two rather large sorely Western thumbs. I felt like a character in a horror movie just before the alien attacks.

We ate an outstanding Moroccan meal of lamb tagine and couscous and then a traditional mint tea before going back to the hotel. I tried my best to keep my mind off of the Twin Towers, the Pentagon and the heroics of passengers on the flight over Pennsylvania, but there it all was, being broadcast incessantly and in living color. Every TV screen in every café we passed, and all of the newspapers on every street corner were delivering over and over and over again the images of the towers falling to the ground, sending thousands to their death. Watching it on TV, it was still difficult to digest that this was stark reality instead. After convincing me to come to Morocco, Fausto started singing another

127

tune. He warned me not to speak too much in English when we were out in public. Even though Morocco was a safe country, it would probably be better to keep a low profile. I thought he was starting to sound a lot like my mother.

The next day was spent meandering around Marrakesh. We ended up decompressing over a glass of wine on a terrace overlooking the main square. We gazed at the seagulls flying overhead. It was the perfect antidote to the accumulation of stress I had been under from first my move, my work situation, my ghastly flat, a long-distance relationship, the feelings of loneliness and the new house purchase; all rendered completely insignificant by September 11th. As the days progressed, I would finally succeed in putting things out of my mind, if only partially. I was helped along by what transpired the very next day.

We decided to take a drive from Marrakesh and up into the Atlas Mountains. We stopped along the way to buy some semi-precious stones that were being sold roadside. The vendor had a pet baboon that was running around accompanied by her two-month old baby baboon. Seeing how cute the baby was, I asked the woman if it would be okay to pet him. She signaled to me to go right ahead, but just as I knelt down to reach for the baby, the mother leapt like a shot straight for my leg, scratching me so severely I started bleeding from thigh to toe. Clearly, it had *not* been okay to pet the newborn offspring of a large baboon. If I hadn't been so wigged out by the vicious attack, I would have thought it totally humorous. Looking back on the entire episode, it seemed like a scene from a Peter Sellers movie when he asks a guy if his dog bites. After he gets bitten, the guy says with aplomb, "That's not my dog." Maybe it hadn't been her pet baboon. I hobbled back to the car feeling sorry for myself, my scarf as a tourniquet wrapped around my leg in an attempt to quell the bleeding.

As for Fausto, a medical emergency meant it was his time to shine:

"My love, the baboon is not a cat—dey are molto pericoloso— verry dangerous."

(*Grazie* for the expert opinion.)

"She wanted to deestroy you because you were stealing her baby."

(Yeah, right.)

"I will repair your leg with the medicine I have in my bag at the hotel, but you need to have your leg disinfected."

(You brought medicines with you? But, of course!)

"The Baboons have many diseases and we need to speak to a doctor."

(Naturally, Italians don't bother eating an apple a day, they simply rush straight to the doctor on a daily basis.)

Once Fausto was assured that I would survive our beautiful day out in the mountain air, our next stop: Fez. Fez is a medieval walled city. Like many grand towns throughout the Arab world, smack in the center of it is a labyrinthine souk. We spent the entire day wandering the streets lined with shop after shop spilling over with pottery, jewelry, antiques, clothes and carpets. Exhausted and overloaded with packages of every shape and size, we returned to our car, but it was no longer where we had left it. Fausto, with his distinctly Roman driving skills, had left his car just like any Roman would have done; smack dab in the middle of a taxi stand. We had been out and about a full six hours and much to our dismay, we found out from one of the taxi drivers that our car had been towed away. As luck would have it, we could take a waiting taxi down to the local police station to fetch it.

At the police station, Fausto and his wacky ways went off as well as an Italian comic in a heist caper. Here he was, one hour into it at the police station and my Johnny Stecchino was still trying to talk his way out of things just like a proper *paesano* would have. *"I geeve you 10 euros and you can geeve me my car back—d'accordo—Eet's a deal?"* I stood by, listening to Fausto try to negotiate a deal for another twenty minutes before he finally gave up. In the end, the officer simply laid out the same procedure he had at the start: he gave us the name of the street where our car was being held and explained it would be about 50 euros, not 10, to get it out of the pound. While Fausto busied himself with the paperwork at the lot, I foolishly disregarded Fausto's 'keep-a-low-profile' admonition and started chatting up the pound owner about our car. Out of the corner of my eye, I could see Fausto imploring me to *"Star zitta!—Zip it up!"*—and fast. I could tell by his facial contortions that he was thinking, *"There goes Chatty Cathy again...Who pulled her cord?"* But before I could put an end to it, the owner asked, "Are you American?"

Unwittingly, and much to Fausto's great dismay, I responded with an adamant, "Well, yes. Why?" Out discharged a tsunami of commentary reminiscent of a school principal with an incorrigible student. "Well, you Americans think that you rule the world—everyone over there is rich *and* arrogant." I couldn't believe my ears. My back arched, I wasn't about to just say, "Thank you for sharing" and move on. I retorted that I was not rich, nor did I live in a big house, and certainly was not as arrogant as he assumed. And, if he must know, I had had a very difficult life. I started working at fifteen in night shifts at the airport just to help my mom pay the bills. In fact, everything I had, I had worked very hard to obtain. It was clear that the pound owner did not want to hear any of it, especially from an uppity woman—and a big-mouthed American one at that. Thankfully, Fausto had the good sense to grab me by the hand and usher me out of there before I was disassembled and sold as used car parts.

All of these hostile encounters. It was quite a slap in the face to someone who always rooted for the underdog, and moreover someone raised in a country she had heretofore believed to be benevolent. In fact, in my American upbringing, I had naturally come to view America as a good country, and Americans the world over as a force for good. The last few days had been a rude awakening. How positively little I knew about the rest of the world. And how even less I knew about how disliked and unwelcomed we were in vast swathes of the globe. I started thinking about what people in other countries actually thought of us. They probably got all of their images of the classic American from what they see on TV. I ran down a short list of American popular culture: *Dallas, Dynasty, Beverly Hills 90210*...it wasn't a pretty sight. It was growing harder and harder to defend my American status, but I was thankful I had been awakened from my deep cultural coma.

After a few more days in Morocco, I went right and Fausto went left. But by this time, at least it wouldn't be another six weeks before we saw each other again. In fact, we would be together the very next weekend. During the course of our two-year relationship, we would make nearly 100 trips, from Tunisia to Thailand, from San Diego to Scotland and of course our weekly commute Rome-London. LAX – FCO – LHR – JFK – FRA—We knew all the airport codes better than we knew our own area codes.

Road to Morocco

CHAPTER X

❧

Two Tails of Two Cities

During my time in London, I attended a black tie event at least once a week. These happenings were always glamorous in the extreme, and though I was quite at ease in any social setting, I sometimes would pinch myself upon crossing the threshold of yet another magnificent venue. The setting, the people, the ambience, the food; they were worlds away from my youth spent in Chicago. It was only when a rice dish was served that I would be transported back to my childhood days when my mother would drench white rice with Ragu sauce and call it risotto. Although I still couldn't bring myself to eat it, being served heaps of rice as a gourmet food at these types of gatherings always made me smile.

Although by this time I still hadn't succeeded in breaking into the inner circle of my own company management, for the first time in my career, people were requesting my presence at one event or another; VIPs hailing across Europe who wanted our business. It truly felt good to be on the other side of the fence for once. Growing up, and given our sheer family size, we were rarely, if ever, invited anywhere. When we were, I can still conjure up the look on the hostess' face when she would throw open the door with a wide smile quickly followed by an audible gasp. There we'd be, eleven eager faces staring up at her, ready to join her child's party. Sadly for us, it would usually be the first and last time she would host the Tondelli's.

All of these propositions filling my social calendar to be seen at London's most 'in' places made the dreadful office drudgery bearable. I felt like a modern day Cinderella: pining away with the miserable stepsisters by day, enjoying a ball with gallant princes every now and again by night. On my own as a globetrotter, I was even starting to build up a terrific group of friends and contacts further afield. I had been seemingly to every capital city in Europe; from Portugal and Spain to Croatia, Germany and Montenegro. I would pass through Paris, take a cruise in Cannes, stop in Budapest, drink shots in Athens, and touchdown in Lisbon, Brussels or Istanbul during the week—making pit stops in Rome to get recharged on weekends. Although it was an exhilarating existence, keeping up this hectic pace was starting to strain the filaments keeping it all together.

Throughout it all, I really missed my two little girls—Thelma & Louise—*The Babies*—kept under the watchful (if not slightly suspicious) eye of their assiduous caretaker, Fausto. One night, I phoned him up and overheard both girls meowing incessantly. Siamese cats are notoriously talkative, but this cacophony was a bit over-the-top. Growing concerned, I finally broke down and asked, "What, exactly, is going on over there?!" My thoughts went straight to worst-case scenarios at the hands of their nemesis: "Were the babies trapped in the small passageway in the hallway? No? Then, what are you doing, torturing them?" *"Oh no, not at all,"* Fausto replied. *"Telma wants more of my prosciutto. And Louise— she is cryeeng out for more mortadella."* I wasn't sure I had heard him right. Turns out, my Serengeti Forest Ranger was treating all three of them to a feast of cold cuts, Italian style. Although I had to chuckle, holed up alone in my miserable little apartment, I was imbibing in yet another falafel sandwich—all to myself. And thank goodness for that. The Lebanese restaurant just up the road was the only place in my area that had takeout food. On most occasions, little did I care that they served mediocre gyros and falafel. It was moments like this that I felt like quitting my job on the spot and buying a one-way ticket straight for Rome. In the very least, if I couldn't muster up the courage to quit, I would take action toward changing my living situation.

Once I started looking at flats for rent in London, it didn't take me long to figure out that it would be cheaper to buy something outright than to rent at the exorbitant London prices. As Fausto had so accurately observed when seeing my tiny rental flat, *"My loooooovvvveeee! You are paying fifteen (h)undred pounds to leeve in a mouse cave!"* The real estate market was hopping, and I soon found a cute and cozy flat in the area of Fulham. My very own place brought with it a glorious feeling of liberation and, despite its small size, creature comforts: I could not only decorate it as I well pleased but at long last I also could bring my baby girls to live with me. It was comforting having a place I could call my own; conferring a note of serenity and sanity in this dreary and damp city on a far-away island I called home. I would no longer feel like such a castaway.

Although I was not settled in Rome with Fausto and the girls, every now and again I stopped to take stock of my situation. Even if I ultimately were to make the move and up and quit my job and go to Rome, I knew one truth: I did not want to find myself totally dependent upon Fausto. I knew that I needed this time in London to catapult my career and in the process, make a name for myself in Europe—on my own terms. And to be honest, I wasn't ready just yet for a full immersion into Italy and Italian life. After my recent failed marriage and living together with guys that fell short in the 'togetherness' department, I wanted to be extra sure that Fausto was truly *The One*. He was Italian, after all, and between my dad, their reputation, and my brush being *Married to the Mob*, I did not want to take this decision lightly. Then again, there were also the practical matters. I still needed to learn to speak Italian, for starters. Incredibly, that stumbling block would prove to be one of my biggest challenges in the entire equation of our cross-cultural contrivance.

I was fortunate enough to find Giulia, a terrific Italian teacher originally from Puglia, who lived right in my neighborhood. Each week, I would spend 90 minutes with her learning grammar and idioms, sometimes touching on cultural differences; mind-boggling details that I would soon discover were more numerous than all the word conjugations found in the entire Italian lexicon. So much for being raised in what we Americans refer to as "an Italian household." Our ideas of Italians back in the USA and those in Italy were like water and olive oil. All told, Giulia diligently busied herself in smartly prepping me for the lifestyle and differences in mentality I would encounter once I left London for good. With every class, I felt I was one step closer to living a full-blown authentic Roman life with Fausto, *La Famiglia* and the rest of the true blue *Italiani*.

From the onset, Giulia refused to speak English to me at all, which helped spur things along for learning even faster. After I had been in London a year, Fausto decided he, too, would refuse to speak in English with me. So between the two of them, I was receiving a major crash course in the Italian language. Past tense, present, conditional, irregular verbs...*ugghhh!* It was like undergoing torture, only in the American sense of the word. Each time I seemed to get something right, a dozen more things would surface that I was getting wrong. After over a year of lessons, I may not have learned a whole lot, but I did develop a profound respect for anyone who could speak more than one language; especially those who had learned a foreign language as adults. By this time, the most I could accomplish was ordering anything in any *ristorante*, especially *pizza, pasta* and *cappuccino*, three words we use in English. Typical American...I just figured that knowing English would be enough to get by. In fact, I assumed that *everyone* spoke English. Traveling around Europe, I found that nothing could be further from the truth. Each time I got off the plane, heck, each time I saw Fausto's own family, I gave myself a swift kick for not having made the effort when I was younger to learn a foreign language.

In time, I would practice my newfound language skills on some of Fausto's relatives. I'd certainly have plenty of opportunities; no one in his entire immediate family, cousins included, spoke a word of English. Trying to make small talk with a cousin who had just returned from his honeymoon, I ended up asking him, "How was your pig of a moon?" I knew I must have screwed up when the entire room exploded in howls. Fausto then said, *"My love, you said, 'luna di maiale' instead of 'luna di miele!' Italian is a tricky language— by changing just one letter you can change the entire meaning of the word...You said 'pig's moon' instead of 'honeymoon.'"* So much for a year of Italian lessons. I wondered if they offered money back guarantees. That same weekend, we went to the corner bread shop to buy our bread. I felt confident enough to try my hand at Italian once again. The woman behind the counter asked me courteously, *"Signora, vuole la pagnotta o il filone?—Would you like the round loaf or the long one?"* Very proudly, and in my best Italian, I replied, *"Prendo la mignotta."* Everyone in the shop, Fausto included, burst out laughing. I kept asking what I had done wrong. Leaving the shop, Fausto explained that I had said that I would "take home the whore." At that point, I decided it would be better to keep quiet until I was a bit more proficient.

After their six-month stint into their Roman holiday sharing salami and meatballs with Fausto, it was finally time for Thelma & Louise to come warm my lap and live with me in my new place in England. I was so excited and had missed them so much—I couldn't wait to come home to my two girls instead of to a cat-free bed in a lonely apartment. Although I had been preparing myself for it, post-9/11, their entry into the United Kingdom was akin to bringing in two jihadists, fully strapped with bomb belts. The first obstacle was the flight. When importing animals, the British regard it as better if your beasts arrive from Germany, rather than from law-bending Italy. So much for the European Union. For the life of me, I could not understand why this rule was in place, let alone enforced. So, off we went, Rome to Frankfurt. Once in Frankfurt, a land of serious rules followed seriously, I discovered that I was supposed to have reserved a space for them on the plane prior to departure. I couldn't simply blithely carry them onboard as I had done back in Italy. In a *deja vu* of their first transatlantic flight, I would have to make a proper reservation and depart the following day. Once again, Thelma, Louise and I would have to spend another night together at an airport hotel, the bathtub serving as litter box.

Just like at JFK, I was not prepared for this small detour, to say the least: Not only did I have no litter box, but no cat food, and who-knows-what German hotel would allow me to bring in not one, but two Siamese cats. Taking a cue from Fausto, I started pleading my case. Miraculously, I was told I could speak to the cargo director in another terminal. So off I went with my bags, and Thelma & Louise to meet the cargo director. Finally, after two hours of tormenting him with my sob story, he finally acquiesced and agreed to let them fly in cargo on the 6:30 pm flight to London that very evening. Another small victory. Rejoicing in my success, how could I have known that the worst was yet to come?

Landing in London, I inquired where my cats had been offloaded. I was told to take a bus to the quarantine animal area. This empire of evil was located about 15 minutes away from Heathrow Airport. No matter, off I went to retrieve my baby girls. Upon arrival, instead of being led over to my cats, I was met by a snarling Englishwoman who acted more like a rabid Rottweiler than a quarantine manager whose sole responsibility is to root out rabies. One word from her and I could tell there was no way a solitary microbe was going to enter her fair land on her beat. She asked to see all of my cats' documents. Confidently, I produced everything I had on the entire UK list. "I have everything in order: they both have microchips, their fox tetanus shots (because you never know when my wild cats will run into a fox in a downtown London apartment,) up-to-date vaccines, the six-month waiting period fully documented, everything." She must have been a pawnbroker in a former life because she ignored my preamble entirely, while scrutinizing the documents without so much as a hint of emotion on her face. For the life of me, I could not determine which way this wordless interrogation was going to go. I prayed it'd go far better than the pearl necklace transaction and silently hoped for the best.

The minutes ticked by. Five minutes, then ten. Terminating her meticulous inspection of clearly what she determined were parole papers for two serial killers, she lifted her head and spat out, "I'm sorry—but I cannot approve the release of your cats." *Whatdaa???!!* Her reason for refusal for entry? My veterinarian had not indicated the *precise time* he gave them the fox tetanus shot. "...Therefore, I cannot release them as we don't know exactly how long it's been since they have been vaccinated." Clearly at the end of my tether, I completely lost it. "You mean to tell me that England, the country of foot and mouth disease, mad cow disease, aviary flu and Lord knows what other life threatening viruses...And you are not going to let in these two purebred Siamese cats who have never gone so far as the living room radiator because you think they are carrying some wildly contagious disease in the span of the 30 seconds it took to receive their shot and the vet registering it??!!" I was beyond livid. I insisted on speaking to her supervisor, but at 11:00 at night I only could deal with this pig-headed, unsympathetic and rabid SS guard. I phoned Fausto PDQ and recounted my latest crisis. I implored, "Please, call the vet's office *immediately* and have him fax over to me the document with the bloody *time* on it!!" Mercifully, Fausto was able to track down his vet at a party. Straight out of a *Seinfeld* episode, the vet discovered that the house he was at also had a fax machine. Between the two of them, Fausto was able to get the required document over to the UK within the hour. God love the Italians and their unbridled passion for working their way around the system. This time at least, I thanked my lucky stars that this was one of their most common traits.

While waiting for the document to arrive, I asked the game warden if I could at least see my girls. She acquiesced, outfitting me as if visiting a power plant after a nuclear meltdown. After getting scrubbed down, I was handed a white janitor's outfit with high rubber boots. Admittedly, though they probably regard the uniform as a serious scientific wardrobe for particle acceleration, I felt like a giant sperm from Woody Allen's *Everything You Wanted to Know About Sex*. Next, I was told to trod through a saline wash solution which led into the quarantine area. Correction: I now felt like Karen Silkwood. Approaching my cats, I passed by monkeys,

139

python snakes, parrots, every sort of exotic beast imaginable. Talk about the Serengeti. I thanked my lucky stars Fausto hadn't been with me. He would adopt this very process for entering his home each evening. Finally, there they were, huddled together in a very small cage, two trembling kitty cats. I could just imagine what they must have been thinking. One moment they were serenely eating *prosciutto* and *mortadella* to their hearts' delight, and the next, they were unceremoniously caged, tossed into a cold, dark, noisy airplane traveling at 500 miles per hour at 30000 feet, only to arrive in a wild animal park with no sign of me nor Fausto to come to their rescue. I could tell they were not so thrilled to see me, knowing full well that it was at my hands they had suffered through this bizarre course of events. At long last, at 12:30 am, the fax finally arrived, the game warden dismissed us summarily, and away we went in a taxi to my flat. The three of us fell fast asleep—all cuddled together in my comfy bed in lonely London. Our six months of forced separation behind England's Iron Curtain was finally behind us. The airlift had been a resounding success.

The following week, it was Fausto's turn to fly over for the weekend. Upon entering the apartment, he greeted the babies with such loving tenderness; picking them up and cooing how he had missed them terribly. Was this the same man who told me that cats should never be allowed indoors, let alone in the bedroom? I started preparing dinner. While waiting for the pasta water to boil, I instinctively began cleaning their litter box. The litter box was stationed smack in the middle of my living room, since my apartment was the size of my Californian two-car garage. Fausto blanched, quickly asking, *My love what are you doing?!"* I stopped myself to see that I was treading truly on very thin Italian ice; what with handling food followed by tainted kitty litter within the same time span and space. Even if I always made sure to wash my hands after each time I pet the cats, I'm sure Fausto would have preferred a surgeon's scrub down at this point. Instead, he remarked, *"You are destroying the babies' toilet."* Well, of course I was. I needed to get rid of the old, and bring in the new. At this point, with the two of us standing over the litter box and both still obviously perplexed, I said, "Sorry, I don't know what you are talking about."

"My love, when you scoop the babies' toilet box, you must be careful not to break the meatballs—otherwise, you destroy their sandbox." Here we go again. Another food metaphor, but this time I told him that the meatballs were on the stove, not in their litter box—and besides, I still didn't understand what he was on about. Like an expert explaining nuclear fission he related, *"You see, the balls of the babies' pee are like leettle meatballs. And you must be careful that they don't finish like piselli—tiny leettle peas."* This was the moment I understood that he was in love with my girls, and that I was falling even more in love with him, if that could have been humanly or humanely possible.

Both of us back at work in our respective countries after our brief weekend interlude taken up by toilet training, I found this message from Fausto in my inbox:

"Sleep well my angel, I am convinced 200% that you are the only woman for me. I also knew many woman in my life and after I shared with you my happiness and some moment of sadness too, I found out what it really could be the pleasure to share the life with somebody, something if I didn't knew you I'm sure I would never have found out in my life. Back in my office again now under the Roman sun after I left you and the babies under the British rain."

CHAPTER XI

❧

To Rome with Love

Time passed, and before long it had been over two years since leaving my family, friends and California dreamland for dreary London. Certainly, being the "companion" of an Alitalia employee had its distinct advantages, but I was starting to wonder if we even truly knew each other; not having ever lived in the same country, let alone under the same roof. By this time, Fausto and I had racked up tens of thousands of miles shuttling back and forth from Rome to London, and countless more for trips back home peppered with glorious vacations across the globe. On top of it all, I had brought in several new clients, had meetings in over ten countries, attended nearly fifty formal events, and had shared precisely two cups of tea with the gruesome threesome.

For someone who had caught the travel bug, with Fausto, you would never have known it. Wherever he went, Fausto would always arrive laden with his personal brand of battle cries. One time, it was:

> *"You know my love, another robbery at the airport! This time, they stole my nails, too! After dey took everything from me, I asked them if they also wanted my underpants!"*

[Upon further questioning, I finally determined that airport security had confiscated his toenail clippers.]

Or another time:

> *"I jumped on dee train like a frog and den I ran like the Incredibile (H)ulk completely sweat until I arrived at the x-ray machine where dare was a Chinese lady ahead of me with many toys in her bag and the belt was not moving, so I climb inside da machine to get my bag and dey almost arrest me! When I explain to da security man dat I am losing my flight he let me go and I arrived (h)alf-naked to da gate. I had my belt wrapped around my neck, my shoes in my hand before the door closed right on my foot. Luckily there was no one on the plane and I ate and slept like the whole zoo."*

Airport and job security notwithstanding, little by little, Rome was calling louder and louder, and we were growing deaf from the uproar. It was finally Easter, 2002 and I had some time off to visit Fausto in Rome. Bored on the flight down, I started thumbing through their onboard magazine, *Ulysses*. Inside, I noticed a small ad for a hotel company based in Rome. At first, I thought that this could be a nice lead for my London architecture firm. But on second thought, it might be a good opportunity for me to unclip my wings, fly the cage and build a nest in Rome with Fausto. Upon landing, I called the company straight away. I managed to land a meeting with *Il Professore*, the Owner and Managing Director of the company on my next trip back to Rome.

On the day of the interview, Fausto accompanied me, briefcase in hand, nervously awaiting the outcome around the corner, as if he were the defense attorney in a landmark Supreme Court case. Like his penchant for wearing smart blazers no matter what the season,

Fausto always carried his briefcase wherever he went. Funny thing though, in all the time I knew him, he never *ever* brought work home from the office. I was fairly certain that there was really nothing of import inside his smart leather bag. In fact, for a red-blooded Italian, bringing work home is considered something just short of blasphemous. In any case, what we both thought would be a brief introductory meeting transpired into a three-hour inquisition. Finally emerging from the building, I told him that I thought the interview had gone well. *"Whatda?? Deed you tell dem your entire life (h)eestoory?"* I apologized for the interview going on so long but all the same, they still wanted to see me again another day. Fausto and I grew giddy from the possibility that a security check-free life together just might be percolating inside those office walls. That night over dinner, we tossed around a Pinochle deck of *What ifs*. Could it be? Could this turn out to be my one-way ticket straight out of London? Ever-practical and evermore superstitious Fausto did not want to jinx the future by planning before it was time. Nonetheless, he did voice his laundry list of everything I'd need in order to set the process in motion to work legally in Italy; from selling the flat in London, to moving into a larger home together, to getting my health certificates to applying for an Italian social security number—all of which sounded a whole heck of a lot easier to say than it would prove to do.

I returned two weeks later for another interview, and, incredibly (and notwithstanding my poor Italian,) they offered me the marketing position with the company. That *Ulysses* ad had shown itself to be another GMC—God-Manufactured Coincidence, as my mother would say! My life as a Roman was finally going to be manifest. No sooner had I stepped off the plane back home from Rome than I put my London flat directly on the market. It then dawned on me that before starting with this Italian company, it would probably make sense to sit down and seriously study Italian. I decided I needed to take a two-week intensive Italian course. I figured it could only help matters, seeing that nearly all the business documents and correspondence would be in Italian, as would be most of the meetings. Not to mention daily life with Fausto. I was filled with equal parts apprehension and excitement.

After months of back-and-forth negotiations and back-and-forth trips, we finally put ink to paper and signed my Italian employment contract. Returning to London, I could hardly contain myself in preparation for our weekly management meeting, relishing the moment I could make my joyous announcement. My heart actually trembled with anticipation as I planned my Great Escape from this miserable hyena's cave. I was nervous, excited and relieved; exactly as I had felt the night I jumped out the window of my dad's home and ran away and into the open arms of Mary Lee. Only this time, it would be Fausto's warm embrace to greet my return from the dark side.

My dad may have welcomed us into his home, but his wife decided she got a bargain deal: two Cinderellas for the price of one. The moment we crossed her threshold she put us to work, using my dad as her task master messenger. Each morning, while his evil wife lay in bed, he would run down the list of chores to be done when we were through with school. Each evening, and even worse than the chores, we'd be prodded by his born-again wife to open up the bible to a random page and read it out loud prior to eating our dinner. On weekends, she would double down on the chores to complete upon return from our minimum wage jobs. The two of us worked on the security staff at O'Hare airport searching for sociopaths only to come back home where we lived with one. We could tell my dad's wife was unstable and that was before we learned that she had tried to kill herself when she found out my mom was pregnant with my little brother. On Saturdays, we'd be up at 4:00 to take the 5:30 am shift. She would sleep in late, only to wake up inspired by a plethora of new chores for us to perform when we got back home.

One morning, my dad started reading off our chores for the day: "Number one, Chris you wash the basement floor, Number 2, Cathy you need to clean the kitchen windows, Number 3, Jenny's pregnant, Number 4..." "Wait, wait, what?!" I gasped. "Can you please repeat number 3?" My father responded matter-of-factly, "Well, Jenny's going to have a baby." True to form, dad, with his abhorrent communication skills, delivered this bombshell with all the warmth and compassion of a sniper let loose in a shopping mall. It was the same cockiness that had stunted his career path and ruined his relationships not only with my mom but with all the rest of us as well. I was fit to be tied.

Shortly thereafter, one evening I opened up the bible and landed straight on the page concerning the *Ten Commandments*. I proceeded to read them out, one by one. When I reached number seven, *Thou shalt not commit adultery*, I pointedly remarked, "Well, now, what do you think the two of you have done?" At that, I slammed the bible shut saying they were both hypocrites and that it was ridiculous that they, of all people, would be preaching this crap to me and I was not going to have any more of it. My father grabbed me by the neck and said we were going for a ride in his car. I thought to myself, "This is it. He is capable of taking me out into a dark alley and just killing me. I'll never be heard from again." During our drive, he told me that he knew that I did not like Jenny, but she was now my stepmother and I had to show her respect. I said I could never respect her for what she had done to my mom and our family. By some miracle, my dad eventually cooled off and we came back home. My sister looked me over for bruises. I felt like a death row prisoner who had just been pardoned. Unfortunately for me, the punishment was yet to come: my dad had gone and told Jenny just how I felt. The next day, she concocted even more ways to treat me worse than ever before. The situation was becoming unbearable and I had to find a way out. I phoned my mom, telling her that I was beyond miserable and pleaded for her to let me come back home.

She said, of course, but that she had hoped we had learned our lesson. I told her I had, adding that there was no need to stay one more day to understand what kind of man my father really was. That evening, I called my sister, Mary, and enlisted her as my accomplice for my great escape. We made an appointment at the stroke of midnight; my sister and her boyfriend would be waiting outside the house in a getaway car. My father would be working and since he never came home before 1:00 am, I knew it was safe. My golden carriage was a brown Trans Am and even though Mary's boyfriend wasn't my Prince Charming, I certainly felt like a forlorn princess being rescued from a cold prison tower. I opened the window, asking my twin if she didn't want to break out with me. She said she could bear the living situation a bit longer and decided to stay. I jumped out of the window holding the same black Hefty bag I had shown up with. It would be twenty years before I would speak to my father again. He forbade me from ever phoning the house or having any contact with my sister again. When I did try to call, he would say he didn't have a daughter named Cathy and would hang up on me. For the next six months my twin and I would meet up after lunch, in between classes and any time we could in order to be together. Shortly thereafter, while watching TV on our living room couch one day, a bullet sailed through the window and I looked out to see my dad's car speed away. All told, it was the most trying period of my life.

Free at last, I relished the thought of seeing my boss hear I was resigning my job and moving to Rome. To my surprise, all three of the directors—the very same stiffs who had tried so hard not to get me hired—appeared actually saddened at the news (or, at least as sad as a stuffed British and American cum English shirt could emote.) They even went so far as to throw me a huge going away party. I considered that in actual fact, it was an elaborate ruse to celebrate my departure instead. On my way out, they told me they hoped I would stay in touch. I nearly bolted out the door, telling everyone that I was finally on my way to *Bella Roma*—for good. I had to start packing boxes and readying my girls to return to the country of *prosciutto* and *mortadella*!

Fausto would come up to help me bring whatever I could manage to take down to Rome. Afterward, I'd be shuttling back and forth until all of my business in London was drawn to a close. Packing up the house, there we were, one big happy family, on our way to live under one red-tiled roof in sunny Rome: Me, with all my suitcases, Thelma, Louise and Fausto, carrying the cat tree under his arm and on board our Alitalia flight straight to Rome. The night before he came up for the final trip, I received this email message from Fausto:

November 15th 2002
My sweet love

Maybe this is the last email I'll write to you, and at the same moment I feel so big happiness for that, I'm also a little sad to lose one of the biggest friend of our love: the keyboard, our messenger angel. She helped us to connect our hearts and minds in the wonderful moments of our life during the last 3 and half years, becoming like a little soft carpet that received the letters as drops of love, and giving also the excitement sensation to send a kiss in one second to the other side of the world. I don't want to say you are the best: you know it already so well looking at the face and listening to the people is losing you forever, but just tell you something people don't know.

Since the first day I met you, you transmitted to me that kind of combination of energy and sweetness that it was then and it is now the food of my soul, without which I would die in a second. The joy and the positiveness you gave me, took me away from an empty life and put me in a gorgeous and magic stay on this planet and right away I understood why it was so easy travel all around the world never feeling tiredness, because the battery to recharge my existence was over there waiting for me.

It's really, really incredible that you are coming here with me. When I wake up in the morning and the first thought is about you, I spend 5 minute to ask me if I'm still dreaming, but after looking at your bag in the living room and the babies it remembers me the gorgeous reality.

I'm almost close to take for the last time the plane to come to you and take my treasure and I wish to say to you for the last time from our messenger angel that seems to cry a little bit, thank you to be in my life and for all the love you gave me. Yes the keyboard is crying like crazy now, but I see someone else smiling in Peace…Roma.

I love you, Fausto

Three months happily settled into Fausto's small apartment in Rome and my London flat still hadn't sold. One fine day, I received a package from my mother. In it, I found a tiny statue of St Joseph whom she claimed would assist me in getting my place sold. Mary Lee would always send her heavenly emissary to anyone in the family who was having difficulty selling their home. She told me that tradition had it that you're supposed to *bury* the poor saint upside down in your front yard, and your home will sell—guaranteed. Seeing I had no front yard in which to inearth the figurine, I took the statuette out of the box and on my next trip to London, placed it right in my front window. Incredibly, my flat sold just two weeks later. Of course, skeptics would remark that it was due to improved market conditions, but my mom and I knew who was truly responsible for my new lease on life!

As soon as we got word, Fausto and I flew in to pack up the rest of the house and orchestrate the move. Always one to tackle any project, from grating cheese to refinishing furniture, with a vengeance, he landed and set out supervising the movers as if commandeering the invasion of Normandy. Fausto ran frantically up and down stairs, calculating the exact angle that the couch could be moved out of my little Victorian flat and through the front room bay window with all the zeal of a tightrope walker. Couch gone, apartment empty, we took one last farewell look at London, ready to bid her a fond *Addio*.

Three Funerals and a Wedding

As soon as I dropped my bags in Rome—this time not to be repacked come Sunday eve—Fausto found me a terrific two-week intensive language school nearby. [So much for the vote of confidence on my budding linguistic talent built up over two years of lessons in London.] I started there right away. Two weeks later, my brother, Phil, came over with a friend. We took them out for dinner along with Fausto's brother and wife at a charming *trattoria*. Thus began our perpetual motion of hosting out-of-town guests. I guess it comes part and parcel with living in the most magnificent

But do we have the kitty litter?

place on Earth. Back at home around midnight that night, I received a frantic phone call from my mother. Choking back the tears, she relayed the tragic news that my eldest brother, Joe, had had a massive heart attack that day, and was found dead in his home. He was only 52. Totally in shock, Fausto and I left the very next day with Phil straight for Chicago to help out with the funeral arrangements and simply be amongst family.

Attending my brother's funeral, I got a glimpse firsthand of just how different our *Americana* funerals were from those in Italy. With Italians, stereotyped as displaying so much emotion and empathy, nothing could be further from the truth. As my entire family gathered in the Chicago funeral home, the scene was one of mass hysteria. [Already a huge brood, and accompanied by spouses and children, there were more than enough of us with Italian *and* Irish blood running through our veins.] Not long before a decidedly different scene had been played out for Fausto's old aunt. Her church service took place in the very parish where her family had been raised for generations. The priest first delivered a very normal (*read:* boring) mass. At the end, and almost as an aside, he happened to mention the *povera* (poor) Maria Rosa who was now being laid to rest alongside her father and mother. Granted, she had been much older than my brother who was cut down in the prime of his life, but really. If it hadn't been for everyone dressed in their Sunday best, and the grim guys from the funeral services gathered in dark glasses to collect the coffin, I would hardly have imagined there to be a prostrate body parked in the aisle right alongside me.

After the priest closed the mass with the traditional, "Go in peace," I hung back waiting for the announcement that the lunch celebration would be at so&so's house or that we'd all be headed over to Orazio's, Fausto's family's favorite place for formal functions, right near the Baths of Caracalla. Incredulously, I stood by as everyone just meandered out, got in their cars and left the premises without another word. My first thought was that they knew something I didn't. Perhaps Fausto just hadn't filled me in on the details. Or perhaps they had made the announcement, but I missed something in the translation. Not only had we not continued on to the cemetery, but there was also no meal planned and no time to grieve or celebrate her life with family and friends who had known her. The feeling was not unlike reading an entire book and finding that someone had ripped out the last few pages.

Looking around the Schmidt funeral home in Chicago, I observed my brother's friends speaking to my sisters, my cousins chatting to my mother, and everyone surrounded by photographs plastered all over the room of my brother's life. In another room just off to the side, refreshments and sandwiches were served in a place to take a break if you needed it. [Leave it to the Americans to make sure you got fed between meals, even on such an occasion.] Heartfelt tributes were made, and afterwards, we'd all be decompressing at a typical Irish wake; the kind that could wake the dead.

In Rome, there was no funeral home, no refreshments, and no interaction between anyone of any kind. I felt as though I was the only one who knew that someone had actually passed away. People simply filed in silently for the formal mass, leaving as quietly as they had entered. The entire experience seemed to me like something straight out of *The Twilight Zone*. Though admittedly, many of my experiences alongside Fausto were always accompanied by this sensation. Fausto couldn't believe his ears when he heard that my Irish grandmother had put money aside in her will to host a luncheon following her funeral for all her friends and family. But this would not be the first of our major life experiences we would have together.

Back in Chicago, in between refreshments and viewing, Fausto proudly told my twin sister that she had nothing to worry about when my time came. In all seriousness, he said there would be a space for me in the Mezzana Mausoleum. At first I thought he was joking, my 'exotic animal' meaning the garden plot where each of the family pets was buried. Instead, he related that his family gravesite was located at *Verano*, the oldest cemetery in Rome. Talk about planning ahead. Given the occasion, my sister and I didn't know whether to be relieved or worried. As was his custom, he offered more gory details than we had asked for: *"You see, Cristina* (he could never bring himself to call her Christine,) *in Rome, in order to make more space in our mausoleum for your seestare, we take dee caskets of the oldest dead relatives and we turn dem on top. If we hear da bones falling down, we take the bones and put in a smaller case. You understand?"* I was wondering if she did. As for me, I started to feel as if I would faint. Oblivious to my discomfort as to where this conversation was heading, Fausto carried on: *"We keep doing dees every 20 years or so and keep putting da relatives in smaller and smaller boxes."* Given the circumstances, my sister just stood there, aghast—obviously not impressed with the Roman cemetery recycling system. In true Tondelli style, she simply turned to him and said, "So, you're telling me that my twin sister is gonna end up in a matchbox some day?!"

A few years later, after Fausto's father passed away, I felt I absolutely needed to have some sort of American-style closure.

Much to Fausto's dismay, and I'm sure that of every family member for generations back and generations to come, I decided to make a large poster bearing photographs of his life. Fausto stood idle, watching me prepare this huge poster board with cut and pasted photographs from his father's life. Unable to contain his curiosity, he finally asked, *"My love—what are you doing?!"* I explained that I am doing what I would do in America when someone dies: put together pieces of their life so during the two days at the visitation, we could all enjoy reliving fond memories of what his dad was like when he was with us. I explained that it helped us with the grieving process and made us remember all the great moments this person had had with those of us left behind. *"Oh no, no baby—tees is verry sweet but you can't bring such a t(h)ing with us! First, dare is no place to put it and seconed, no one does dis in Eetaly—dey will not understand."* I told him I didn't care and packed my oversized poster board in the car. I was determined to bring some sense of honor and celebration to what I thought would be the funeral home. Much to my horror, I was totally confused when Fausto pulled the car up to the local hospital. *Whatda??!!* As we walked down the cold, sterile halls, I could tell we were following signs for the morgue. I was glad to be in a hospital because I thought I would die of heart failure right on the spot: Images of being greeted by Quincy himself pulling open a drawer, and us saying our goodbyes to a frozen stiff.

Arriving at the morgue, we found Fausto's father laid out on what looked like an ambulance stretcher in a room so small, we had to file in one at a time. To add insult to injury or, just to make sure St Peter had a full schedule manning those pearly gates, we even had to share the miniscule room with another family that had just lost their beloved mother. Like a scene from the *Godfather*, people from both families mournfully filed in, pretending to ignore the unknown dead person in their midst, all the while talking in hushed whispers. I looked around. No place could have been more aseptic nor less comforting save for a few miserly bouquets of flowers placed around in order to cover up the fact that you were actually in a gray hospital room with lousy fluorescent lighting overhead.

Without a word, and ignoring Fausto's remonstrations, while soliciting a host of curious looks from Fausto's family (not to mention from his dad's roommate's family as well), I unabashedly put the poster board up on a table just by the entranceway. At least for one visitor, it would be comforting to see photos of his father in happier times during his life. People stopped a moment to gaze at the photos as if eyeing a strange fish in an aquarium. They would look around as if they might be caught debasing themselves; distracted as they were in their mourning by the pictures on the board. Pushing my luck, I asked if I could take the poster board to the church as well, so that everyone else could look at something a bit more uplifting than the bleak hymn book. Clearly, I had stepped outside Italians' *Bella Figura* (putting your best face forward) boundaries. The entire family looked at me as if I had come from another planet. It was another *Mork&Mindy* moment. Except this time, *I* was the one regarded as the alien life form. The conversation was cut short by the *Men in Black* who informed us we had only one hour left to say our goodbyes. Clearly, like turning tables at a local eatery, they needed the room for the next ones to arrive. So both families paid our last respects rather quickly before the sun-glassed thugs straight out of *The Sopranos* put him in the casket, flowers arranged at his feet (where onlookers could see them clearly through the back of the hearse window) and drove him over to the church. Naturally, no one, not even his wife of 57 years, grieved openly. And as far as I could tell, nor did the husband and family of his roommate, either.

It was through sharing life's little events and those much larger that Fausto and I were growing used to each other's bizarre ways. Our imperfect union certainly had its ups and downs, but little by little, we found we were comfortable in the other's nuances. Fausto was *"molto particolare"* (a terrific term meaning 'very particular' that Italians use for someone who's a bit persnickety) and liked everything in its proper place. An American would most likely come to regard him more like someone suffering from OCD—Obsessive Compulsive Disorder instead. As for me, Fausto found my habit of having music blaring whenever I was at home completely off the charts. And he would always wince at the fact that I happily shared my living space with my pet cats, no matter in which part of the house I was. Despite having fallen in love with my babies, for him, house cats were still of the same variety as the mangy ones circling the streets of Rome.

One day, when we were both at home, Fausto suggested we go to the park. In his peculiar parlance, he actually put it to me as, *"Let's go out of doors and take a walk—we must profit from this beautiful day."* Naturally, he used the charming word, *profit* whenever he meant *take advantage of* something. Living in Italy, both words were actually appropriate; Italians always seemed to want to take advantage of something or someone at the slightest opportunity— for some personal gain. As we were walking, he turned to me and said, *"I teenk we need to teenk about the beeg question."* By this time, I was quite used to his poetic metaphors peppered with drama, so I immediately set the wheels churning on deciphering his romantic code. Aware of my bewilderment, and cognizant of the gravity of the situation, he ventured into unchartered waters for an Italian: putting something to someone straight with no circuitous reasoning, no mystical metaphors, if he was going to get his message across to one straight-talking American. He made his pronouncement loud and clear: *"You know, my love, I have been teenking for a long time now…and I teenk it's time we get married."* Although my heart started to quicken, instead of being overcome with joy, I stood there, paralyzed by fear.

Fully embraced in a *fight or flight* response, racing through my mind were a thousand conflicting thoughts. They ran the gamut from my parent's marriage (or rather, their separation) through to my own unlucky trials at marital bliss, straight down to all the couples I knew who were truly happy in this institution: I could count them on one hand. At the same time, I knew I had never felt like this with anyone in my entire life. But that beautiful, hesitant moment of tenderness was soon eclipsed by all the reasons why I would never want to spoil something that was working out so well. And then there was the wedding itself. I couldn't think of a worse curse to put on a couple seemingly in love. I'd been through the ritual of choosing a wedding dress before, of having to deal with relatives who don't agree on the menu, of hearing someone complain about the music selection, someone else about the food, and worse, the chorus of comments over the guest list and why Aunt so-and-so had not been invited not to mention the countless fist fights that transpired at almost every Tondelli wedding. Coming from such a large family made the outcries all the more audible in my mind. Imagining all of this *and* across two continents, I thought I would nearly pass out from the very notion.

In the grip of full-fledged *Friday the 13*th scenes of terror, my awkward silence was made all the more boisterous in reply. Finally, Fausto simply took my face in his hands. He then whispered what I am sure will go down in history as the most curious marriage proposal ever: *"My love, I understand if you are afraid...You have done this before and it didn't work...But don't you remember? We are two lions, and I could never be with a sheep. I need to be with my lioness forever. I am ready to be leenked to you, like two leenks in a chain, my heart to your heart. Do you understand, my love?"* I was at first amused by his animal analogy, but I then hoped he wouldn't be thinking he was chained down like a wounded animal just a few short years ahead.

Sister Act

Heading back home, dizzy from the ride through the Tanzanian bush, and slightly dazed by the prospect of actually settling down with Fausto at long last, I knew what I had to do: call my big sister, Renee. Whenever I was going through one crisis or another, she was the one I turned to for advice; always on hand to talk me down off the ledge. As the eldest daughter, she was tasked with helping to raise us younger ones. But growing up, I could never have known just what similar paths our lives would take. Over the years, I found I could always count on her sage advice to talk me through yet another breakup or business deal, as if she were talking someone down Mt Everest in a snowstorm. And with the flurry of conflicting thoughts all clouding my head, I certainly was in need of steady footing.

Renee had the curse of being born the first girl, a novelty after three boys. But her place of honor also had its hardships. My father was extremely protective over her, and he refused to let her go out of the house, let alone with boys. Whenever he found out that she had been out on even an innocent date to the movies, she, or the boy she had been with, would get a slap down. Fortunately for the rest of us, Renee as a result had become quite adept at taking care of the wounded; nursing everything from bruised heads to hearts. When I had surgery, she was the one who came to stay with me during my recovery. Calling her up, I couldn't believe my ears when she told me that she would be working on a film in Italy, and would be coming over for three full months.

Renee's arrival couldn't have come at a more portentous time. I quickly filled her in with the news that Fausto had just proposed marriage, albeit in his very Fausto way. That he was ready to trade his life of roaming the African savannah to live with his lioness in a more tranquil habitat. She asked me what I had said in reply. I told her that I hadn't, actually, coughed up as much as a modicum of a response. In actual fact, my reaction wasn't like most women in this circumstance. I hadn't jumped up and down, Tom Cruise-style saying, "Yes, yes! I've been waiting for this day forever!!" On the contrary, I stood there shell-shocked, with no vocal cords to vibrate even a murmur of reply. Furthermore, before I did answer, I would really need a healthy dose of moral support. I already had been down this route before. I simply didn't want to make the same mistake again. Why couldn't we just continue living together? She convinced me that my feelings were completely normal, adding, just for good measure, that she had never seen me happier with any other man in my entire life. Thank God for big sisters.

CHAPTER XII

～

Home Improvement

After thirteen months together in Fausto's miniscule bachelor's pad (roughly the size of my master bath back in San Diego), the very one he had been closing on four years prior and just after our fateful meeting at the *Trevi Fountain*, we thought it was time we bought a place of our own. It was hard to assess just what a whirlwind these last four years had been. Across time zones and continents, tripping over customs, language and cats. And then there were the unimaginable miles, the romance, the miles, the jobs, the miles, the apartments, the miles, the family, the cats, our diverse backgrounds and entire ways of living. Heck—even our noise levels were sometimes cause for compromise. [Fausto lived in low decibels, I and my raucous family were larger-than-life.] Nonetheless, and in no time at all, we had found the perfect apartment in a tidy suburb close to Rome, nearer the airport to ease

Fausto's commute. Finally, we'd have our very own place we both could call, *Casa Dolce Casa*.

But first, I would need to sell my home in San Diego. Back then, Italians needed to put upwards of 40% down payment on a house. Between Fausto's tiny apartment, and my having just cleared the mortgage payment on the sale in London, San Diego had to go. I was fortunate to have my mother living nearby, and one who happened to sport a realtor's license. Little did I know my house sale would ultimately come down to a typical *Tondelli Family Affair*. After years of renting the place, and with renters still living inside, it was proving a tough sale. So tough, in fact, that even St Joseph couldn't work his magic on it. In short, the house wasn't doing so well for the wear; it was getting rundown by the tenants, and it showed. On top of that, my present tenant had a giant Doberman and two small kids inside; not the ideal conditions for arranging an open house. It would take nothing short of a miracle to find the money to buy our new home.

Incredibly, the moment Fausto's apartment sold I received an offer. My mom and stepdad acted as my realtors. Although I accepted the offer, I still needed to pass the inspection. I had a sickening feeling that my place would never make the grade. My mom ran down the laundry list of items that might trip things up, any one of them a deal breaker: the boiler had to be replaced, roof tiles were broken and the outside deck was rotting through and needed to be refurbished completely. On top of that, the Doberman had eaten its way right through the front door. I would need a heap of good luck and barrels of money just to make the place shipshape prior to the inspection. I had just two weeks' time.

Knowing that even Saint Anthony wouldn't be able to find me an extra $10,000 and a home builder in that amount of time, I did what anyone else in my family would do in times of crisis: I called my brother, Jimmy. If Renee mended hearts, Jimmy was the one who mended the fences. From the time he was eight years old, he showed an aptitude for these sorts of things. He had been watching my dad lay tile in our downstairs staircase. After about fifteen minutes of seeing my father struggling to figure out how to lay the corner pieces, my brother picked them up and said, "*It's just like a jigsaw puzzle—you need to cut the pieces like this.*" From that day forward my dad had anointed him our absolute in-house genius, and Jimmy became the family's go-to guy for just about everything. He was the official *Consigliere* of the family; acting as lawyer, realtor, notary, mentor or anyone that served to get any of us out of a jam. Not only would he come riding to the rescue, but he also had the gift to make people believe he held the pedigree of whatever profession we needed at any given moment. It helped that he was movie star handsome and, a Jack-of-all-trades. Once, when half the family had gotten into a rumble (over an ex-boyfriend, no less) they were taken down to the clinker, including my mom. It was Jimmy who showed up posing as the family lawyer to get them sprung from jail. He actually had licenses for just about everything; everything, that is, except the title of 'Esquire'. In my eyes, Jimmy was a cross between Leonardo da Vinci and James Bond.

I called him that Monday evening to see if he could save the day once again. Without a word, like the Lone Ranger and Tonto, he and my nephew took off into the horizon to help the damsel in distress. They turned up the very next day at the house with tool belts and materials in hand. He had to work hard to meet the inspection requirements for the closing that Friday afternoon. They worked tirelessly for three full days repairing holes in the doors, replacing the rotted deck boards and taking care of the other two dozen items on the punch list. Needless to say thanks to my brother, we passed the inspection with flying colors. Back in San Diego, Jimmy has created his very own slice of Italy that he fondly calls *Toscandido*, replete with a tiny *piazza* in which to pass lazy afternoons watching the sunset, while savoring the gorgeous red wines from his vineyard. Not only had he grown a thriving vineyard, but he also planted olive trees and an organic fruit and vegetable garden, and built himself a villa from floor to ceiling; sewing all the curtains in the house himself and even painting the frescoes inside. If only his lovely vineyard were here in Italy, we could have raised our glasses to toast the success of the sale on account of his handiwork.

On the day we put the down payment on the house, I caught sight of Fausto with one of his customary looks of sheer panic across his face. By this time, I knew to take these looks with a huge chunk of salt, knowing his tendency for adding drama to any situation, no matter how great or how trivial. But instead of breaking into his customary whirlwind of words and motion, this time, things were different: he was stone silent. I said, *"Che c'è?—* What's wrong, my love? Are you sad to be leaving your apartment, your brother, your mother?"* By now I knew that in family-oriented

Mary Lee & her legacy

Italy, it's considered a huge feat if you leave the actual family home to take your own place—right upstairs. What came next made me guffaw outright: *"You are so calm,"* he told me. *"Don't you have some preoccupation about our move, our new home?"* I failed miserably trying my best to rise to the seriousness of the occasion. He then asked me how many times in my life I had changed houses. I started counting them out, figuring it was about 27 moves when I decided to cut to the chase and answered, "I don't know exactly, but probably about 30 times." This, of course, provoked Fausto's familiar response, though his hint of incredulity had risen to new dramatic heights. *"Whatttdaaaaaaaaa???!!"* By this time, everyone in my entire extended family had adopted this expression to great effect.

"Okay, okay," I offered, taking things down a notch or so, "I don't know exactly (making a concerted effort to lower the count, lest it sound far too outrageous for his Italian synapses to process.) "Maybe 27 or 28?" I began running through the umpteen moves, apartments, houses and cities in which I had lived. "Let's see, born and raised in Chicago, that's at least five right there, not counting going from place to place when the house burned down…various apartments in college, four moves in San Diego alone, Rogers Park to Park Ridge, Elk Grove to Long Grove, and of course, the detour to a farm in Texas…" I asked him how many moves he had made in his lifetime. Now it was my turn for *"Whatdaaa?!"* Whereas I had moved cities, states, even countries, for an Italian like Fausto, he was adventuresome—venturing so far as right across the street from where he had been born and raised.

In fact, with this immobility came one of the biggest challenges about making a new life together in Rome. Romans never leave. As a result, there is little to choose from when it comes to finding an available apartment. Should you as a homeowner decide to rent out a place, the good news is your tenants never leave. Except the bad news is…they never leave. You practically need a papal decree to kick out a lousy tenant. The upside to all of this, of course, is that you don't find yourself always changing carpets nor splashing twenty coats of whitewash over walls that someone painted fire engine red. Fausto, always quick to up the ante on his already outlandish stories, went on to tell me that he once knew a person who actually placed a bomb in his rental apartment in order to avoid being thrown out. In fact, Fausto had been a renter in his apartment for ten years before the owner decided to sell it. This was Fausto's great fortune. In Italy, rental properties must first be offered to the tenant. And when the guy died suddenly, post-purchase agreement signature, well, Fausto was able to buy it, no strings attached. He had made the down payment for the closing the day we met. I always like to think that he started building his foundation on the very day I gave him title to my heart.

That evening we went over to see his parents. One look at the two of them and I quickly deduced that they, too, were teeming with *ansia*—anxiety over our having put a down payment on a home. It was then and there I realized that I needed to step in and perform an intervention to get the entire Mezzana family over this impending life transition. Fausto overcame his fear by way of reassuring his mother that we weren't actually moving to Siberia, but only 20 minutes further from their home. I could tell by her reaction it was more or less tantamount to the very same thing. I offered up for good measure that it took me 20 hours to go and see my mom…so what were 20 minutes? At long last, their spirits lifting, we promised that we would come and visit them at least every other weekend.

At least initially, Fausto's apartment sale had been a breeze; a breeze at least until we fell face-first flat into the quagmire of Italian bureaucracy when it came to transferring title. Within hours of putting the apartment up for sale, Fausto was contacted by an Italian woman whose two daughters were attending university nearby. Fortunately for us, student dorms in Italy are few and far between, so she wanted our apartment for them to share during the academic year. As part of the sale agreement, however, Fausto had arranged a deal that would allow us to stay in the house until we were able to close on our new place and move in over there. Unfortunately for her, things didn't go so smoothly for *La Signora Morante* and her daughters. They ended up having to sit on the sidelines for nearly eight months before finally taking possession of our apartment. Our new house had a lien on it. In actual fact, we would discover there were two liens. It had been repossessed by two banks simultaneously, the owner just centimeters away from filing foreclosure. Because of the complications involved, Fausto had to peruse every detail, speaking to countless attorneys, notaries and consultants before putting any money down. Italy is rife with tales of people losing their shirts on muddy or on downright dirty real estate deals. Although judged to be a prime piece of risky business, he felt confident we could go through with it anyway.

In the end, Fausto's parents needn't have fretted: from the time we set our sights on what was to become our new home, nearly an entire year of back-and-forth negotiations between buyers, bankruptcy judges, new tenants and old, would transpire before the day finally arrived to complete the closing on the house. After so many years apart, and so many trips just to find the time to be together, I couldn't believe how our wayward paths had finally converged to bring us and keep us together. We had clocked roughly fifty-two trips per year, plus extra travel for vacations to destinations near and far, and adding in our respective globetrotting on business, it was nothing short of a miracle that things were still on the right track. Despite all the turbulence, both literal and figurative, the ease of our cross-continental relationship had been pretty smooth sailing. Having grown up with so much drama in my life, I reveled in the familiarity and routine of Fausto's family life. And even with his singular penchant for making mountains of molehills, those episodes would usually leave me reeling in fits of laughter. With Fausto, laughter was our daily bread, while nights were spent enjoying good food, good music with Fausto serenading me on the piano, or just talking the hours away. Everything was going swimmingly—if you don't count the unfathomable magnitude of stress of severing apron strings, that is.

Finally committing in writing to a lifetime together in our very own abode, the subsequent closing took place in a nondescript room of the *notaio's* office. We took it as a good omen when we met an elderly woman in the waiting room there. She asked us how we had met. When Fausto replied, *"At the Trevi Fountain!"* she replied, *"Bravo! You managed to catch an American? You must be one of the finest fishermen I have ever seen!"* Unfortunately, for all concerned: the sellers, the buyers and the two of us, we would be swimming upstream from there. The closing that ultimately unfolded came off like a scene from *It's a Mad, Mad, Mad, Mad World.* Two bankers were present, each one armed with a lien on the house we were purchasing. One by one, the rest filed into the tiny office: two judges, two lawyers, one notary public, the buyer of Fausto's place, her daughters, their two bankers, and the owner and wife of what was to be our new home. While we pored through our purchase agreements, the former owners would be carrying out their own foreclosing procedure simultaneously. All eyes were fixated upon the two of us at the center of this bureaucratic bazaar. It took the better part of an afternoon, complete with espresso bar breaks, until all of the negotiations, the mountains of paperwork, the dozens of signatures, and the exchange of bank checks was finally at hand. With a nod from the head notary, we were signaled to go through with the final formality; the passing of the house keys to the rightful owners across the table, signifying possession. It was as lofty a moment as when the priest asks you to exchange rings after your vows. I was fully expecting the *notaio* to say, "You may now kiss each other as a sign of your everlasting love." If everyone hadn't looked so serious, I could swear we had been filming an entirely Italian slapstick comedy.

Keys to our new home in hand, now *La Signora Morante* only needed us to abandon our premises. Although it was in both our interests, this particular task made cleaning the Augean stables pale by comparison. We would not be ready to move out completely until our new apartment was fully remodeled and in move-in condition. Anywhere else, this would seem like something no sooner said than done; not in Italy, where nothing is deemed urgent enough to be accomplished in a hurry. On top of everything else, we were now heading straight into summertime, where the living is easy; we would need to allot double the time for any works that might take place when all of Rome took off for the seaside. It was mid-June by the time we hired a carpenter named Stefano. He had been referred by a neighbor and, more importantly, was willing to work through his precious summer days. Stefano started in earnestly, tearing apart floors, walls, electrical wiring, heating elements, you name it. Clearly in the dark about remodeling work in Rome, we had notified *La Signora Morante* that we expected to move out around the end of July. She agreed, and like a super on a skyscraper development, would phone us each and every week to check on how the work was progressing on our place. I personally believed she kept tabs on us to make sure that we hadn't simply skipped town with all her money, and the apartment still in Fausto's name.

Fausto would pass by the new place sometimes during the day and on most evenings to check on Stefano and the work progress. He also wanted to make sure that the remodeling was being carried out to his liking. He would phone in daily reports. *"Today I had a meeting and my boss asked why I had snow on my shoes. I must be careful to clean my shoes tomorrow, so that he doesn't see I am stealing time every day to control the workers."* I asked him what he meant by snow on his shoes. *"You know my love, the snow from the floor and all the pollution that they are making in our house."* I understood that he meant the fine white powder from tearing down all the plaster walls.

Come August, the work still wasn't complete. Fausto told me that Stefano had asked him for an advance on payments for August. He said it was because he wanted to take his mother away for the major holiday in Italy on August 15th, *Ferragosto* or Feast of the Assumption. He said he needed the money upfront so that his poor old mother would not be left in the city, all alone. Naturally, in Italy, a country that places *La Mamma* above even the Pope, this was not an outlandish request. We agreed, and gave him an advance of 1500 euros. With no work going on, we left for the week as well. But upon our return, and after dozens of phone calls, left messages, and attempts to lure our Stefano back, it was clear he had taken the money and run—decidedly without his *mamma* in tow. We would never see him nor our money again. His poor old mother was probably left to rot at home in the scorching heat while he was living it up at a beach resort with some hot babe. We should have known: the whole shenanigan came straight out of the film, *Pranzo di Ferragosto.*

High Anxiety

In the meantime, *La Signora Morante*, who decidedly had *not* gone on holiday with her mother nor the rest of the Romans, was anxiously waiting for the go ahead on her own move. She naturally wanted to make absolutely sure her daughters would have a place to live come September. Adding to our distress, we discovered that finding workers in August in Italy was like trying to find a Honeybaked Ham on Easter Sunday in the Bible Belt. We spent the entire month of August searching for someone, anyone—not to pick up the slack, but to pick up the phone. Finally, we found a company willing to do the work—but only starting September. They would be more costly than sleazy Stefano, but at least we could trust that they would get the job done quickly and not pull off another *Italian Job*.

With each passing week, *La Signora Morante* was growing justifiably more and more impatient. She started threatening to hire a lawyer to get us evicted out of her apartment once and for all. Of course, we both knew that any lawyer worth his salt would be on holiday 'til September, so time was ticking to our metronome. Fausto reassured her repeatedly, telling her that surely by the end of October her daughters would be happily ensconced in their Roman bachelorette pad. This seesaw of back and forth negotiations between Fausto and *La Signora Morante* were actually nothing more than smokescreens; part and parcel of the Italian psyche. When it comes to exchanging words, Italians, when their feathers are ruffled, tend to be melodramatic; raising their voices loudly, gesticulating wildly. But in the end, after the dust has settled back down, they simply go for a *caffè* together and act as though nothing happened. This feature of Italian life always reminded me of episodes of *Tom and Jerry*. But what *La Signora Morante* didn't know is that nobody had the gift for linguistic sparring like Fausto, and nobody but nobody could out-dramatize Fausto in the drama department.

It was on one such occasion that Fausto was having a meltdown at home. In a frantic state, he interrupted an important business meeting I was in, saying he absolutely had to speak to me urgently. By now familiar with his tendency for overreacting to minor stimuli, I cautioned him that I was with four important hoteliers, but if it were truly an emergency, I would leave the room immediately. Totally up in arms, he assured me it was a *"liivve-tret-ening situation."* Excusing myself from the room, I was now in a panic as well. I stepped out asking if he had gotten into an accident. *"No,"* he said, *"Much worse!"* My brain ran through the entire gamut of possible catastrophes. Did his mother die? Or—*heaven forbid*—one of my cats? The list was endless. He impudently went on to inform me—standing outside the door of my meeting, dumbstruck from what I was hearing emanating through the phone—that our cleaning lady had left a bottle of Viakal cleanser on the marble countertop in his bathroom. It had left a permanent ring and in his mind was completely destroyed. With no accompanying apology for his ludicrousness, he asked innocently, *"Do you know what dees means my love?"* In reply, I told him in no uncertain terms that frankly, not only could I have cared less, and that I could not only not believe what I was hearing, but should he <u>ever</u> call me out of a meeting for such an "emergency" again, he'd better make darned sure there was a dead body and investigators at the scene, or else there would be one later on that evening.

Illness of course, was the apotheosis of all dramatic incidents. Early on in our life together I was cognizant that I would never ever be a match for his *mamma's* level of ER administration when it came to a case of the common cold or an onset of the flu. It just wasn't part of my makeup to be, shall I say, utterly paranoid about whatever life or death condition had come on. In Fausto's world, stomachaches out-trumped all other illnesses, and with them came the greatest amount of TLC, but not from me. About the time he turned stark white after hearing of my brother-in-law's vasectomy, he would remark, *"I was <u>dying</u> and you stay behind to feenish your dessairt, leaving me alone with dat terribly old woman. Only when you were done did you come to see if I was still alive or dead!"*

It wasn't until mid-November, nearly eight months after our circus closing that we would finally make the move into our new house and, to our mutual relief, *La Signora's* girls into theirs. The move for me was anything but stressful. I was going to be settling into a new life with the man I truly loved. Once again, Lady Luck was on our side. The proprietor of Fausto's tiny apartment had been an avid antiques collector. Moving things out to move into our new home, we ventured down into the storage unit. There, we were amazed to find a small treasure trove of rich furnishings: a Merano glass chandelier, a few pieces of 18th century furniture and some paintings worth thousands. Not only that, we discovered volumes upon volumes of antique books. It took us three trips to the Rome library to donate the volumes our benefactor had collected over the years, and we still had enough to fill the new library of our new apartment.

Still, blithely packing boxes as if I hadn't a care in the world perplexed Fausto. Preparing for the move brought back memories from the time my mother made the move of her lifetime; supposedly to start anew with the man she loved. My father had sold our house right out from underneath us, moving us to a 13-acre farm he had bought in Texas. He told my mother that he would move down to Texas as soon as he found a job playing jazz music there. Surrounded by cowboys and country music bars, it came as no surprise to learn that he never did succeed in finding a nightclub gig playing Chicago jazz in Denton, Texas. Not that he tried so hard, either. In the years we were down there, he barely managed to put in an appearance. Eventually, he moved all the boys back up to Chicago, stating emphatically that *Little House on the Prairie* life was meant for girls. Even with half the kids up north, he still managed to spend time with his bride-to-be without being disturbed by the rest of the brood. For those left behind in Texas, we made the most of it. Who'd ever have thought that a born-and-raised city slicker like Mary Lee could morph into someone who could live off the land? Or, in the very least, try to. Under my mom's enterprising supervision we learned to be totally self-sufficient. We used the pecans and peaches from the trees on our farm and grew our own vegetables. My mom rented out part of the property to cattle herders. We grew accustomed to stopping in at 'fire outlets;' places where they'd ship food and clothing for sale from stores that had burnt down. I imagine that that's where the term *Fire Sale* came from. We gals even learned to do the two-step, further adding to our dance repertoire. After our neighbor's dog had puppies, we begged our mother to let us have one. She finally relented, but ever-practical Mary Lee, just so we could use him as a herd dog to move our cattle. We named him Ragù after the brand of spaghetti sauce sold in jars; a fitting name for a hound dog belonging to an Italian family from Chicago. After leaving Texas to move back up north to Chicago, it was clear that Ragù simply couldn't adapt to city life. As for us, right upon our return, my father fessed up and asked my mother for a divorce. It turned out that it wasn't only Ragù who couldn't adjust to the new life ahead. I prayed with all my heart that this move would be a great deal more promising.

For fastidious Fausto, the actual *trasloco* (move) itself provided fodder for another one of his legendary anxiety attacks. Once again, it was not over the details surrounding the move itself, but over my sheer calm when it came to such life-changing events. Unfortunately for him, our move ended up being scheduled the same week as my brother Reno's wedding. Seeing that there was no way we could put off *La Signora* another day without being served with legal papers, we decided I would fly out to California myself, leaving poor Fausto to orchestrate the entire move all on his own. Given the circumstances, and the general tsunami of emotions running through Fausto's bloodlines, I determined that for my part, this was one time that a large family had its distinct advantages. Although even I had to admit, uprooting our two lives to move into our new home was one instance where a classic Fausto panic attack would be fully legitimate.

I Want Someone to Eat Cheese With

Having finally put the move behind us, we started building our life together. On occasion, this signified purchasing items for our home. Like many Americans, I would also give into the temptation of buying items that we really didn't need, but that I simply liked to have. In the U.S., I always had an available garage and lots of storage space, so even if I didn't need something, I would buy it and stick it or the thing it replaced somewhere else. One could say that this wholly American ritual of spending Saturday afternoons in Pier I or Pottery Barn and coming home laden with trinkets was almost part of my DNA. But it hadn't always been this way for me. Once, when I was about ten years old, my teacher gave us a project to construct a Christmas tree out of gumdrops. She told our class that we needed to buy a

Styrofoam Christmas tree, along with a bag of gumdrops and toothpicks for decoration. That evening, I told my mom about my school project and asked her if we could stop in at the store. She told me flat out that I had to go to school the next day and inform my teacher that we simply didn't have the money to spend on these sorts of things. The teacher would just have to understand that we had eleven kids and I could not be expected to participate in projects involving the purchase of auxiliary art supplies. I was overwhelmed with embarrassment when I showed up at school the next day—none of the art materials in my bag. When my teacher asked where my items were for the gumdrop tree, I replied that my mother said we could not afford them. Everyone in the class started to laugh. My teacher tried not to make an issue out of it, allowing me to sit with another kid in the class to help her make her tree.

In apartment-living Italy, I was little by little coming to the realization that this wholly American art of consumption needed to be reigned in—and fast. Not only were the homes entirely of a different breed, but they also came with furnishings and home décor passed down for generations. Their frugal furnishing model seemed contrived to keep your spending habits to a minimum, even in the stores themselves. Across the narrow boot of Italy, not only were the stores infinitely more cramped, but so were the tiny baskets you carried down the aisles; only slightly larger than a basket you'd strap on the front of your bicycle. I found myself always thinking twice before putting anything in there. At the grocery store, my range of decisions were downgraded from American-style 'family-sized' portions to weighing out whether I would rather fill the space in my Lilliputian refrigerator with a single bag of lettuce or one ball of fresh *mozzarella*.

One afternoon, I went out to Italy's version of Target and bought some candles, vases, throw pillows and a few other sundry household decorations. As I walked in the door carrying all my bags, I could tell by Fausto's bulging eyes that something was amiss. Immediately thinking it was a case of indigestion, what with his fragile stomach and all, I inquired, "Are you okay?" "*Well my love, I see you are eating all of our cheese.*" Once again, with his Cheshire

Cat delivery of riddles, Fausto's comment elicited my very own and now all-to-common response, "Whatda??!" By way of explanation, he started regaling me with his roundabout reasoning, which always took twisted turns around the true meaning while never failing to contain a reference to food. *"Well, you know...we (h)ave only one block of cheese. And you are taking beeg bites of it and in a few years, we will have no cheese left."* Not being Italian, and not used to solving brainteasers during my daily routine, I took it at face value. I innocently charged back with, "Are you speaking about the mozzarella that I bought this morning? I mean, I could buy another mozzarella ball if you don't want to share it with me..." Despite our years together as a couple, I had yet to catch on that Italians never meant what they actually said; that there is always a hidden significance behind almost every word that passes their lips or they read in the newspapers. It's the stock that made Umberto Eco and his *In the Name of the Rose*. Fausto then struggled with a form of American directness; attempting in vain to hone in on what it was, exactly, he wanted to convey. *"My love, what are een all dose bags you are breenging into our (h)ome?"* Finally brought around to his line of thinking, I understood that he didn't think my shopping bags were full of cheese rounds that I had taken a sudden urge to nibble. Figuring out at last that his line of questioning was not about cheese at all, but about money, I cheerfully blurted out, "But, I didn't go shopping at Fendi, my love, *non preoccuparti—* don't worry, even with all this stuff, we will still have enough cheese to last us for a few years." Eureka. I was satisfied with myself that I was able to converse on the level reserved heretofore by Cicero.

But just when I thought I had broken the code, Fausto decided to up the ante: *"My love, eet's not only the cheese dat you arre eating, but we have no place to put all disa stuff you keep breenging (h)ome!"* Living frugally. Not one of those terms in the 'Ugly American' spendthrift lexicon. It was clearly time to face the fact that I was an unrepentant shopaholic. And I now had a new home in which I could direct my purchasing power with the skill of a tennis player making a tough corner shot. Poor Fausto. It would take a few years more to break me fully of the shopping habit. But I now think twice before putting another lamp, picture frame, or vase in my shopping cart. Living in Italy, and living with Fausto, I have learned to live more simply and have become quite adroit at maximizing my living quarters so well I could compete with any Italian *Signora* who came my way.

As we learned day-by-day to ride the waves of our relationship more smoothly, my Italian lifestyle was becoming easier for me to navigate as well. My Italian was growing more proficient and I even managed to jump the pirate ship of doom that had brought me to Rome in the first place. I had started work at Charming Hotels, a misnomer if there ever was one, at least in terms of their management style. Before seriously considering walking the plank, out of the blue I was thrown a life preserver; once again while attending a conference, this time in London. I scrambled aboard and found myself finally working for a superb U.S. company that allowed me to cast my net throughout Europe. Off I'd go, content with the knowledge that Thelma & Louise were being looked after with love and care by their benefactor, Fausto. I was dressing more like a European woman, and even with my blonde tresses, people rarely pegged me for an American, a particular point I was quite proud of. On plane trips, I would leaf through the Italian gossip magazines and striking up conversations with movie stars and businesspeople who always took me for an Italian at first; that is, until they heard my Midwest twang. Regardless, I was really starting to blend in; something that in a post-9/11 world was important for me as an American broad abroad. Fausto's flexible schedule, the airline benefits and his maniacal cat management expertise made it even easier for me to go home to the USA every now and again to spend time with my brothers and sisters and mom whenever I felt homesick. It was on one such occasion that I told Fausto that I needed to spend at least a couple of weeks in America. He told me to take as much time as I required.

Even though I lived in Italy, a place with the finest food on God's green Earth, I still found a few items from my American lifestyle missing: those very favorite foodstuffs that only Americans could concoct. Trips home to the USA meant carrying an empty suitcase so I could bring back all of the delectable American delicacies I couldn't find easily (or so inexpensively) in Rome: spices, Toll

House chocolate chips, real vanilla extract, evaporated milk, pecans, Hershey's syrup, and good ol' Kraft macaroni & cheese. My suitcase would serve up a virtual smorgasbord of American comfort foods. On this particular trip, I had stocked up on my winter inventory of Kraft macaroni & cheese, making sure to pack all the boxes at the top of my suitcase so they wouldn't get too smashed. It was one of my all-time favorite American foods and also served as a quick dinner when I was home alone and feeling homesick. Not only would the mac&cheese not go bad until I reached retirement, it was also a bargain at 99 cents a package. Arriving in Rome from my peculiar international shopping spree, I looked out the airplane window to see nothing but torrential rain. Fortunately for me, this was an uncommon sight in *Bella Roma*. Deplaning, however, we had a very long wait for our bags, due to a *sciopero* or strike of the airline baggage handlers, which unfortunately *was* a typical feature of the Italian landscape.

Waiting for my luggage in arrivals, I saw Fausto making his way over. As an Alitalia employee he usually was able to talk his way into the baggage area. This time, after a whole 45 minutes, my bag shot out from the carousel—completely drenched. As it hit the edge of the carousel, I could see a huge orange stain soaked through the top of my bag. Giving Fausto an inquisitive look, I informed him that my bag wasn't orange when I had left Los Angeles. He went over to the Roman luggage handlers to ask what had happened. They replied that many of the bags ended up sitting out in the rain longer than usual as a result of the strike. We quickly opened up my suitcase to root out the cause of the orange tint. To my horror, or rather, to Fausto's, I discovered that *every single one* of the boxes of my mac&cheese had been so thoroughly soaked through, they had torn wide open. Inside, a king's banquet of miniscule macaroni was strewn throughout my case, limping from the rainwater. As if I were a victim on *Candid Camera*, we found the bright florescent orange cheese powder had exploded in flight, conferring a bright mandarin glow on my underwear and tennis shoes. My thoughts went to how many great inventions started out as mistakes, and maybe this would be one of those instances: me, the inventor of clothing and cosmetics good enough to eat. Fausto took one look at this blinding tangerine explosion and couldn't contain himself: *"My love—I do not understand. You leeve in da contree of pasta and you bring two tons of macaroni from America??! Are you completely crazy?!"* I simply sat there transfixed on what had been a virtual mac&cheese fest, just in case the candid cameras were, in fact, rolling. I may not have been on TV, but I had attracted quite an audience. There I stood in the Arrivals zone, over an open suitcase bursting its seams with glow-in-the-dark pasta surrounded on all sides by dozens of onlookers and an irate boyfriend. Granted, at face value, Fausto certainly had a point. Perhaps I was truly "carrying coals to Newcastle." From that point forward, I never brought macaroni & cheese home with me again. And even though Fausto is correct, to this day, you still can't find that kind of macaroni & cheese in the entire Italian peninsula.

Settled back in at home with Fausto, I related just how much I had enjoyed spending time with my family. Nonetheless, it was becoming more and more clear with every trip back home that I was feeling increasingly more at home in Italy than back in America. Although I missed my family terribly, it was growing more difficult for me to imagine ever moving back to the USA. On flights bound for the U.S., I knew my Italian lifestyle would be very hard to replicate, or even to afford in America. The idyllic life that Fausto and I were carving out for ourselves seemed straight out of a romance novel of international jetsetters. Our summers were spent traveling to marvelous island destinations, each one absolutely brimming with Old World charm: *Ischia*, for the hot thermal baths, *Ponza*, once a tiny fishing village, *Favignana* and *Ustica*, volcanic islands off the coast of Sicily. During the daytime, we would comb the island or take boats out and go fishing. Evenings we spent relaxing with a good read, lounging on a terrace, or dining out on another superb fish dinner, always followed by a chilled glass of luscious *limoncello.*

Italians make it a national pastime of eating out. For them, first comes family, then church (if they are practicant), followed by holidays and eating out. But for many Italians, it seemed to me that the pecking order was reversed. Either way, it didn't matter much to me; all I knew was it was a terrific departure from how

I had been raised. Brought up on a shoestring, restaurants were totally out of the question. Our annual family vacation consisted of one day spent at a local beach on Lake Michigan, splurging with a trip to McDonalds. And even then, the price tag on an order of over 30 hamburgers and a dozen packs of fries caused their registers to quiver. The few occasions that my mother packed us all in the car for an outing were marked inevitably by one of us left behind. My poor sister, Renee, after seeing to it that the little ones were all snugly packed in, would be left curbside time and again. Eventually, we would turn back, finding her standing on the street corner, waiting patiently for the moment when someone finally took notice, shouting out the familiar, "Wait! Where's Renee?!" Once, though, after about 15 minutes in a big warehouse store, my mom noticed my sister, Andrea, was no longer part of our troupe. She tore through the store every which way to find her, finally spotting her walking out the front doors, hand in hand with a "nice man" who had offered to "buy her some candy." Needless to say, after that episode, my mom never took the lot of us out at the same time again.

In the winter, Fausto and I would venture off to ski in the Alps or the Dolomites, to places like *Cortina* or *Selva Val Gardena*, or around *Mont Blanc*. The rest of the year, we would take trips to the Umbrian or Tuscan countryside, or spend lazy days surrounded by the olive groves outside Rome with friends or family, or delight in strolling the streets of Rome savoring our creamy *gelato*. Fausto would always tell me that I was a *gelato* addict, or as he put it, "*You are drugged by gelato!*" He didn't know how much of an addict I truly was. My love affair with ice cream started when I was about seven years old. Each day, we kids would have to do chores. And while I'd be busy vacuuming or dusting the furniture, my sisters would often burn up the couch cushions watching TV. As soon as they heard my mom's Cutlass pulling up to the driveway, they'd shut it off and get working. But my mom was always onto their ploy. She'd walk in the door, head straight for the TV and like Leona Helmsley, give it the white glove test. But not for dust. She'd feel for heat emanating from the back of the tube. Seeing me hard at work (I confess, I was always a kind of neat freak), she would whisk me out the door and to the local ice cream parlor for a big ice cream sundae, just dripping with hot fudge. Digging into my dish, I could never comprehend why my sisters would ever prefer TV to a sundae, but in that moment, I didn't care. Once I moved to Rome, I found that American ice cream didn't hold a candle to the scrumptiousness of Italian *gelato*—it was undeniably ambrosia, food of the gods. I made it my personal mission to carry out my very own personal focus group; trying out every single flavor in every single *gelateria* in town, in order to identify the ultimate taste sensation. I would try a new *gelateria* almost every day that I could. I hit the triumvirate of flavors with the toasted pistachio from *Giolitti*, the incomparable *cioccolato* at *Venchi*, and the luscious cherry cheesecake from the *Teatro Gelateria* near *Piazza Navona*. I went through withdrawals whenever I had to leave town, until finally forced to wind down my insatiable search for the most exquisite flavor in Rome once my clothes started feeling snug around the hips. Say what you will, but in my book, consuming a huge dish of ice cream at the end of the evening was the consummate symbol of opulence.

When Fausto first took me on those resplendent trips during our courtship, I merely thought they were the enjoyable outings that one did when newly in love. Instead, my fairytale life with Fausto was actually a fairly typical way of living that many Italians grow up with; but one that Americans only dreamed about. I loved every moment of it and wouldn't give this splendid lifestyle up for all the tea in China, nor for all the *gelato* in Italy.

My Beautiful Laundrette

Especially after the *Great Mac Attack*, it sometimes seemed to Fausto and me that those tiny fissures in our cross-cultural relationship might actually be as wide as the Grand Canyon. Often, it was the little things, like salad-eating behavior: I preferred to eat my salad *before* the meal, or to eat a huge salad *as* a meal, and, in the very least, to put cheese on my salad, inevitably be served *after* our meal. But Italians have *highly* strict rules governing eating, foods, mealtimes and drinking. From a foreign perspective, they seemed

178

to be the only rules that Italians followed with an almost religious fervor. For Fausto, the salad came decidedly after the meal, pasta *was* a meal, and grated cheese was for putting on that very same pasta dish—and on nothing else.

Once, I came home to discover Fausto going through all of the items in our kitchen cupboards. He would examine each item with the meticulousness of a biologist looking for Ebola virus cells. One by one, I watched him toss out all of the goodies that I had brought over so assiduously from the United States; inventory for my personal drugstore. Here he was, fancying himself as a purveyor of all the items I simply couldn't live without. Examining the expiration dates on my baking soda or vanilla extract, out they'd go. In Fausto's mind, they were germ-infested bacteria refuges, ready to attack everything and anything that might come into remote contact with so much as the packaging. I told him that in my lifetime, there had never been a single, solitary case of death-by-expired vanilla extract. My pleas for salvation were cast off just like the goods themselves; I stood by helplessly as I saw my baking endeavors headed for the trash. Other times, our tiny differences could turn into huge rifts, all for lack of cultural understanding. These situations would usually come to the fore particularly after one of my trips home from the USA. While doing the laundry one day, I was overjoyed to find that Fausto had bought a new washing machine while I was away. After years of using a washing machine with practically two settings only (on & off), I couldn't wait to give it a whirl.

They say that the washing machine was the one item that revolutionized the western world. It singlehandedly liberated women from the slavery of hours spent trying to scrub the dirt out of family garments (and back then, families were as large as my own.) Well, whoever said that was only half right. Because they neglected to mention the 'dry cycle.' In Italy, finding a dryer in a home is as rare as finding a funeral home. Surely, this practice was steeped in tradition. In fact, why would anyone want a dryer when they had kilometers of clotheslines hanging from one building to the next or extended across every balcony in the *Bel Paese*? Other apartments managed to install the technology update and had clotheslines

179

hanging on the wall above bathtubs. Fausto claimed that no one had dryers for the same reasons that households didn't overshop: lack of space. That, and the expense of running the darned thing. In Italy, electricity costs about five times what it does in the USA, so people use it sparingly. In a country as traditional as Italy, new technologies were also suspect. People believe that dryers suck the color right out of the clothes; others claim (rightfully so in cotton and linen-laden Italy) that the dryers shrink garments to gnome sizes. While these statements all bear a hint of truth (a telltale sign of an urban myth), based on my decades of experience in a rather large family of thirteen, I can swear on a stack of bibles that no one's clothes had ever been shrunk in the dryer, and any fading came, in fact, from the gallons of cleaning agents tossed mindlessly into the washing machine.

My sister used to call our clothes cleansing outpost the *Tondelli Chinese Laundry.* The eldest girl, Renee, was the self-appointed manager of our enterprise. Each and every day she would bark out the orders, assigning us laundry duties. We'd trudge down the basement steps to be met with a virtual mountain of clothes that had been sent down the laundry chute. "Chrissy you fold, Mary you iron, Andrea—you're in charge of the washer and dryer." Banished to the basement, we would entertain ourselves between loads staging full-length Broadway shows or plays. It was just one in our repertoire of inventive ways we'd amuse ourselves, along with outfitting competing sides for a soccer match or a baseball game. Growing up, we didn't have money for board games or Barbie dolls, so there we'd be, reenacting *Tom Sawyer, Hello Dolly!, Annie,* and even *Seven Brides for Seven Brothers.* Our troupe certainly could manage to fill out all the parts. Theatrics aside, life wasn't much better for those who made the cut up above. Upstairs, my mother ran our household with the precision of an army platoon. Each day, we had to check our chores posted on the wall. "Tonight, Chrissy you set the table, Mary you clear the table, Cathy you wash the dishes, Andrea you dry. As usual, it was the boys who generally got out of doing their fair share, and it was Renee who decided she was second in command. Much to our dismay, she did not shy away from pulling rank. Needless to say, I still dislike doing laundry to this day, even if it's my own.

In any case, I couldn't wait to use our new *lavatrice* (washing machine). For the christening, I had settled on doing a load of whites. In my enthusiasm, I tossed in a pair of pink underwear that I didn't think would make one hoot of a difference. That evening, Fausto came home to find his brand new, white D&G shirt hanging in all its perfectly pink panache on our drying rack. He took one look at it and turned a few shades pinker. He vowed that from that day forward, *he* would be the one on laundry duty. After all was said and done (and believe me, with Fausto, it was quite a mouthful,) this was nothing short of a godsend. My days of forced labor working down the basement in the *Tondelli Chinese Laundry* sweatshop folding, ironing and washing more clothes than in a real Chinese laundry, what with their one-child policy, had come to an end. I could honestly attest that, yes, indeed, washing machines had given at least one woman a whole new lot in life.

CHAPTER XIII

⟨⟩

The Wedding Planner

$\mathcal{I}$t had been only a few weeks after Fausto had asked me to marry him [clearly taking my stone silence for an emphatic, "*Sì!!!*"—Besides, even if I'd had said "No," he would have surely let loose an entire battalion of persuasive arguments to make his case in true Italian style; they never ever take 'no' as a proper reply.] We had been invited to a small village about a two-hour drive from Rome, located near the once papal city of *Viterbo*. We had joined a small group of investors who were looking to renovate the tiny medieval hamlet of *Vitorchiano*, eventually selling parts of it to wealthy foreigners. My big sister, Renee, had come over that week to celebrate her 50th birthday, and she and her boyfriend tagged along with us on the tour. The village was a walk into the past; a charming yet simple place housing ancient buildings made from tufa, a type of grey peppered lava stone, delightful fountains and the best pizzeria in all of Italy, *La Grotticella*. Strolling leisurely around this enchanting 13th century walled village, Renee convinced us all that it would be the perfect place to hold our wedding.

That night, we had dinner in a small sort of gourmet inn, the *Locanda di Sant'Agnese*, formerly an austere convent that once housed an order founded back in the 1300s. The monastery itself had its origins in 1466, continuing to expand and improve throughout the subsequent centuries before falling prey to more secular norms; it was transformed into the site of the small luxury hotel it was today. We got there by way of Fausto's customary stratagem whenever he found himself in a new place. Wherever we went, he would unfailingly stop to ask an elderly village matron where she would suggest we go to eat. Four years on, and his tactic had proved infallible. Over dinner, we admitted we were love struck with the town as well as the *Locanda* and determined that very evening that this would be the place where we would be married.

The next morning, as we strolled out into the small *piazza* in front of the hotel, we spotted a stunning 12th century church. I couldn't help but think that it was another GMC moment. It was perfectly situated only about 20 feet from the convent! We set across the *piazza* to go and meet the priest and tell him of our intentions. We were greeted by one of the nuns who said that the priest would only be there the following day. So, we decided to 'profit' from this occasion and spend another night in lovely *Vitorchiano*. We went out for an absolutely heavenly pizza at *La Grotticella* before retiring early. We were brimming with excitement to meet Don Alberto the very next morning and finalize all our plans before making a mad dash back to Rome. It seemed to all of us that the stars were aligning quite magnificently to shine upon our imminent wedding.

The next day, we met with the owner of the 16-room former monastery. Totally trusting that we were doing the right thing, we were even so bold as to book all the rooms immediately, along with the reception hall and pizzeria from the night before. *"Eet was our strrange destiny,"* Fausto exclaimed, *"Proprio strano destino!"* This time, even I had to admit that finding ourselves in *Vitorchiano* was an unexpected hand of fate, pure and simple. In fact, it seemed to me that the only peculiarity in the unfolding of our nuptial plans was that things were going off without so much as a glitch. Energized by the serendipity of each event, we waltzed into the Church of Saint Agnes (which sounded a lot better in Italian, *la Chiesa di Sant'Agnese*). It was quite a sight to behold, with the morning rays of sunlight beaming straight down upon the altar. We took this as yet another sign that we had found the ideal spot, indeed. "*Buongiorno, posso aiutarvi?—May I help you?*" piped up a gritty voice that seemed to have come straight out of nowhere, and that echoed through the church. Turning toward its source, we were met by a pale, elder sacristan whose sole purpose was to mind the church. He looked like he had never once left the place to see the light of day. Fausto explained that we had come to meet with Don Alberto, but perhaps we were a bit too early. The sacristan cordially replied, "In fact, he hasn't arrived yet, but I will take you to his office."

Waiting there inside the office of this little gem of a church, I began biding my time perusing the priestly collection of books and crucifixes and poring over photographs of the last few popes hanging on his wall. Fausto upbraided me for being "*molto Americana—such an American,*" (and when he used this epithet, I knew he was not paying me a compliment.) He told me to mind my p's and q's seeing that the priest most likely wouldn't appreciate me snooping around his office. "What? Isn't this what they're there for? Why else would he have so many books and objects right here on display?" I shot back, sitting back down just in time for Don Alberto to walk through the door. "*Buongiorno, sono Don Alberto,*" he said calmly. He was very friendly even as he probed our true intentions. He started by inquiring if we understood the commitment of marriage and the deep significance that God plays in carrying out a successful union. I imagined that he just wanted to make sure we weren't tourists who fell in love with the place and decided to marry there at the spur of the moment as if we had been passing by the Elvis Chapel in Vegas. I supposed that in Italy, this might happen a lot. Instead of discussing the ways of the cloth, however, I replied with my usual banter and running off at the mouth on just how beautiful the village was, the convent, the old walls, in an endless river of consciousness commentary. Fausto quickly interjected, trying to cork my unbridled stream of thought, saying politely more to me than to Don Alberto that actually, we didn't have much time to talk, since I needed to get back to Rome

185

for my weekly meeting. By now, Fausto knew how much I took after my mother in the gabbing department—hours could pass before I might realize just how much time had run out on the clock.

"Allora," Don Alberto started in: *"Then, let's go over what you will need in order to have your wedding in the Catholic Church."* Taking out a piece of paper, he asked, *"So, you both have been baptized?"* "Yes," we replied in chorus. *"Good. What about your first communion?"* We both shook our heads, yes. *"And, of course, you will have to bring in your confirmation certificate as well."* Always at the ready, Fausto promptly replied that he would bring it to him the following week. Suddenly, I felt two sets of prying eyes upon me. I drew a blank and instinctively flashed a big smile. Most likely, I would have to dig mine out from the boxes in our basement where I kept all of my old papers and photographs. Finding me suddenly speechless, Fausto grew concerned, pumping me for information. *"Well, my love you do (h)ave your confirmation chertificate don't you?"* As if it was the most natural thing in the world to produce on a moment's notice just like a driver's license. I had absolutely no idea—and truth be told, I wasn't even so sure I had ever even made my confirmation. There had always been so much chaos in our household, and I had been to so many communions and confirmations of brothers, sisters, cousins and their offspring, that for the life of me, I truly couldn't conjure up the memory. I told the priest that I would need to phone my mother later that evening and we left it at that.

Prenuptial Tango

Back home, I called my mom asking her if she could possibly recall my making my confirmation. I might as well have asked her how many times all us kids had come down with a case of the flu. I realized from her reply that my request was tantamount to trying to retrieve the proverbial needle from her 11-kid-high haystack of coming-of-age events. "Well, honey, I have to think about this. You know, it was a long time ago and after eleven kids, I have a hard time remembering who had chicken pox, who had measles, who made their confirmation and who didn't." Down but not out, I realized I would have to dig into the archives of my own faulty memory bank. Mary Lee, trying to be helpful, urged me along: "Don't *you* remember, honey? You would have had a sponsor and you would have worn a white dress." So this is what the rite of confirmation boiled down to? Nothing. "Well, then, you were never confirmed," she said judiciously, shutting out the one glimmer of hope I held to seal the deal.

We phoned the priest the next day, and I told him that to the best of my knowledge, I had never been confirmed. There was no way around it, he said, I needed to have proof of my confirmation in order to be married in the Catholic Church. This was one instance in which I couldn't count on a GMC intervention—How ironic, I thought, seeing that this very conundrum *was* with the Catholic church itself. Not only would I need to take confirmation classes, Don Alberto explained, but we would have to attend evening pre-marital classes as well. These would be group classes with other prospective couples in order to learn the ways of matrimony. [As delivered from a group hailing from a pool of celibate and single men, but hey, who was I to argue?] Completion of our holy matrimony coursework came with official certification that we had achieved marriageable status within the church protocol. I wondered what it meant if we didn't pass the course with flying colors. Were we to try again? Or perhaps, break up? Disheartened by the very prospect of carrying out what for me were starting to look like Herculean tasks, I finally looked at Fausto and popped what to me was *The Much Bigger Question,* when it came to affairs of the heart, namely: "Would your mother be terribly disappointed if we didn't get married in the Catholic church?" In reply, the color simply drained from Fausto's face to the point I thought he might have to be carried out on a stretcher. I surmised that that option was totally off the table.

The very prospect of sitting in a class for thirteen weeks with a bunch of pock-marked and PlayStation-happy 13-year olds to discuss the bible was about as miserable a prospect to me as facing the gauntlet of interviews I had with my former company directors I had left behind in London. I felt as though I was looking at being thrown to the lions for my beliefs. We decided to discuss our spiritual dilemma with *La Mamma* of Fausto. Seeing her hopes about to be dashed for her little *bambino* (never mind he was already

50), she said she would speak to her parish priest the next day about finding a solution. Fausto's pious *mamma* went to church every single day, and made a confession at least once a week (about what, exactly, I would love to know.) If anyone could find a way around the church directives, she most likely could. True to her word, she phoned Fausto later that evening and said that they had come to a *compromesso* (compromise). We could have six private sessions with her priest, in lieu of attending the six-week marriage course. As far as my confirmation certificate was concerned, however, there was no way around it. I would have to tote my Bible in a backpack with the best of the tweens. Relieved, we called this the *Historic Compromise,* after a dark chapter in Italy's history when Italy's prime minister decided to negotiate a deal between left and right wing factions—although later he was found dead in a car trunk for his deed.

We went to *La Mamma's* church the very next day to thank the priest and—bringing out the best in Faustian fancy footwork—to make one last-ditch attempt to get around the confirmation certificate as well. If I followed the dictates of the church, I would never complete the course in time for our wedding. Incredibly, and like almost all the other rules in Italy, we found there was some elasticity here, too, but only so much. The priest offered, *"Because your mother is such a good Catholic* (so much for confessing a pirate's bounty of sins), *and because I have known you and you family for so long, I will agree to sign a declaration allowing you to marry—on condition you enroll in the confirmation class after your wedding."* He then presented me with a sort of prenuptial agreement that I had to sign. I quickly inked my name to this 'promissory note' to take religious classes as soon as feasibly possible. I felt like I had just passed into the lead on the game board of *Life.* Wedding bells would be ringing from the church tower, without the certificate. It would be one of the very few times I would admit it, but I had to thank God for Italian *mammas.*

Marriage, Italian Style

After months of preparation and planning, the Big Day or rather, the wedding week of events had arrived. Fausto remarked that once his family had read the matrimony itinerary we had plotted out over the course of a few days, no one would want to show up. He was certain that our guests would be *completely destroyed* just from reading through what they were supposed to be doing in the name of our union. In his humble opinion, it was an Iron Man contest at best. The Italians weren't used to a multi-day matrimony, a typical feature of the American wedding landscape. But with guests coming from far and wide, we all couldn't wait to revel in each other's company for days (and nights!) on end. We had planned for the occasion special events in Rome, the wedding in *Vitorchiano*, and then a trip through Umbria. In the end, even Fausto had to admit that it was fitting, after so many trials and tribulations, to make the most of our first days as the lion and lioness in the company of our entire pride.

Guests poured into Rome from across the globe, while others headed up to the lovely walled town of *Vitorchiano* to sightsee and relax before the big day. The celebration of our wedding would actually begin two evenings beforehand, at the *Basilica di Santa Maria sopra Minerva* right in the heart of Rome. We had chosen this particular place to hold a special service with close family and friends and presided over by our parish priest inside the private Chapel of the Sacred Heart.

The Basilica had a significant meaning for the two of us and we had asked Don Alberto if he would bless both our houses for the union that would take place two days hence. Both the Tondelli and Mezzana families congregated in the quiet *piazza* where Bernini's elephant stands guard. We all filed into the Basilica, under its cobalt blue vaulted ceiling, representing the heavens. There, we were met by Don Alberto—keys in hand—who opened the iron gate of the tiny chapel. Placed prominently over the altar is one of the most important paintings by Fausto's grandfather, Corrado Mezzana; a depiction of Christ between Saint Catherine of Siena and Saint Margherita Alaquoque. In fact, my mom and I had made a point to visit this very church on our fateful trip four years earlier. She had wanted to pay her respects at the tomb of Saint Catherine, from whom I get my name, situated at the foot of the altar there. When Don Alberto pronounced his blessing over our upcoming nuptials, we all could feel the eyes of generations of Mezzana's, those with us in body and many others in spirit, smiling down upon us.

We were also blessed by the balmy Roman weather and leaving the church, we headed straight up to the enchanting rooftop terrace of the Hotel Minerva just across the way. A brilliant orange and red Roman sunset lit up the sky, leaving a golden laminate upon the church spires and rooftops and reflected in windows and across the dome of the Pantheon nearby. We may have started out the evening in the traditional Mezzana way, but now it was time to party into the night, in true Tondelli style.

The next morning, the entire wedding party (in more ways than one) would head up to the convent hotel and get settled in for the following day's festivities. It did not get lost on the participants that Chatty Cathy had chosen a convent for her new life as Fausto's spouse; after all, our word *cloister* comes from the Latin, *claudere*, meaning to *enclose* or *to shut up*. Was I supposed to take this on as a talisman for marital bliss?! I'm sure on most days, Fausto would appreciate the gesture. Arriving at the hotel, we were guided up to a stunning room with a view overlooking the terracotta rooftops in this charming medieval town. That night, our expanding wedding party took over the pizzeria for more revelry and good times. After dozens of bottles of wine, even language barriers seemed to be broken with everyone chatting wildly and gesturing away with gusto. Our last night spent as an unwed couple was together—we figured that at our age, pre-nuptial superstitions were well worn away for them to have any effect.

"Lei è arrivata!—She's arrived!" exclaimed Fausto's old aunt who had been standing sentry anxiously at the back of the church. I was outside, just behind the immense, age-worn, wooden doors. They opened slightly, and out came Fausto to take my hand and escort me down the aisle. The last time, this honor was bestowed upon my brother Jimmy. On both occasions, I certainly couldn't have counted on my dad to lend me an arm as I met my betrothed. Fausto, for his part, wanted this moment to be ours alone; just the two of us, hand in hand. Bride and groom together, with closest friends and relatives as testimony to our love was for both of us the most beautiful gesture of our unity. Once we reached the altar, we exchanged our own personal vows in Italian with me stumbling through them mispronouncing every other word despite weeks of practice. My poor performance

notwithstanding, it seemed it was only a few moments until we were finally united—*marito e moglie*, husband and wife.

As we walked out of the church, we were met with pure pandemonium from townspeople and guests shouting from all sides, "*Viva gli sposi!—Long live the bride and groom!*" A rather large crowd of locals had gathered in the *piazza* to see the *Americana* marry the Roman. I saw it perfectly fitting that in Italy, they still threw fistfuls of rice; the very kind used to make the repulsive *risotto*. I think it was at that very moment, having undergone a sort of baptism by rice, that I started to learn to love the dish. That night, we raised our glasses time and again to our love, to "strange destiny," to our families for being so supportive all these years through all of our trials. For Fausto's *mamma*, I don't know what was worse: our living so far away in another Roman neighborhood, or her *bambino* being forced to live out his life in the company of my wild animals. We reserved a special toast, of course, to my mom, Mary Lee—for having chatted up my future husband initially in front of the fountain and later coercing me to go for a ride in his car. But especially for so bravely enduring his inimitable driving (and parking) skills. We even gave up a special heartfelt toast to Alitalia, without whose generosity for allowing unmarried and unlimited partner travel, our relationship would never truly have gotten off the ground.

As I took a look around to take it all in, I scanned each of the people who had made this fairytale possible: my mother who said she "Would have flown halfway round the world not to have missed this day" (and, in actual fact, she had), my entire family except for my brother, Tony, who, unable to travel said he'd be there in spirit, my closest friends from across the U.S., Italy and even Debra the office receptionist from England, and especially, my new Italian family. All together, we walked across the *piazza* and over to the monastery to celebrate with champagne served in the cloister's stone courtyard. The town *piazza* had a lovely fountain right in the middle of it. As I passed it by, I wondered just what might transpire if someone had three coins to toss right in.

Wedding Risotto

Le Nozze Di Mezzana

∞ The Mezzana Wedding ∞

Cathy, the Queen of marketing and sales, won a trip to Italy,
once upon a cold November.
First class to Venice, Florence and Roma,
a trip she always would remember.
She stood admiring the Trevi Fountain on this, her next to last night
While a handsome Roman named Fausto was keeping her in sight.
She reached for three coins and turned around
to toss them over her shoulder,
Making her three wishes known just like everyone had told her.
"Scusami, Signorina," the handsome Roman pursued,
"You must toss them over the other shoulder
for all your dreams to come true."
"Wow," she thought, "this fountain sure works fast!"
Soon they were sharing pasta, their single lives already in the past.
Back in California, hours on email and the phone just weren't enough,
They missed each other terribly; it was getting to be too tough.
Falling ever more deeply in love, the phone bills soaring high,
She began to think the time had come to bid America goodbye.
She was offered a job in London and started looking into flats,
But first she needed to talk Fausto into taking in her cats.
"My love, the management of the Babies is a big responsibility,
I don't think they would want to live in Bella Roma just with me."
But alas, poor Fausto, in the end he really had no say,
The Babies come with Cathy—there simply is no other way.
At first they were little "criminals," getting into everything,

But six months at Camp Mezzana and the Babies began to sing.
Life in London wasn't all it was cracked up to be,
Bomb threats and no Fausto, it seemed like an eternity.
"I want you to come to Roma, live with me and be my wife."
So she got a job with the Professore and embarked on her charming life.
Enjoying their life together, dining, dancing and sharing showers,
Poor Fausto just wasn't prepared for the arrival of the Towers.
"My love, your feet are so petite, but your shoes they are so many.
Do we really need the hallway stacked with closets filled aplenty?!"
But like the Babies, Fausto learned that heels are a necessity,
Cathy, the Babies and her shoes, well it's almost a holy Trinity.
She adores his family, and also so do we—they really are a kick,
When in Roma we all look forward to the showing of the Brick.
We're very happy they met that night over scoops of sweet spumoni,
Saving our beloved Fausto from becoming (gasp!) a Mammone.
Addio a celebato, Addio a nubilata, and
Benvenuto from all the Tondelli's,
*We promise, Fausto, we will do our best to never Romperti le Palle! ***

*Scusami = Excuse me
Addio a celebato/nubilata = Say goodbye forever to bachelorhood
Mammone = Mamma's Boy
Benvenuto = (a warm) Welcome
Romperti le Palle = Break your balls
Poem written by Renee

About the Authors

This is a debut novel for Catherine Tondelli, who is still very happily married to her wacky husband, Fausto. They live in Rome with her two Siamese cats, Louise and the latest addition to the family, Stella, while Thelma is buried in the Mezzana family pet mausoleum outside Rome. When she's not taking fabulous vacations or entertaining friends in Rome, Catherine spends her days working as an Events & Meetings expert with luxury hotels and globetrotting to and from special event venues and hot spots in various locales. Catherine is always on call to find just the right spot to host a conference, a seminar or a cocktail party atop a Roman terrace offering a breathtaking view. After 13+ years with house pets, Fausto now lets Stella cuddle up to his face but in true Italian style, the bed is still reserved only for humans.

Catherine Tondelli c.tondelli@alice.it

American author Francesca Maggi has been an active blogger since 2007, which served as the inspiration for her book, Burnt by the Tuscan Sun, offering a hilarious look at Italians' most well known and steadfast cultural idiosyncrasies. She works as a multimedia content editor & producer living in Rome and publisher of a series of audio guides and apps to Italy's most amazing places. Maggi has ghostwritten and edited a number of books, articles and websites,  including a bilingual series featuring Italian contemporary authors. Living in Italy for 20+ years, her goal is to visit every single town tip to toe of the Boot along with her dog, Trevor.

http://burntbythetuscansun.blogspot.com
http://www.touringtracks.com

**Me, Fausto & Mary Lee getting ready
for another nighttime tour**

*Just when you least expect it, life throws you a curve ball, spinning you
in a different direction than you ever thought you would go, opening a
door to a new adventure, down a new path and over to a new life.
Take my mom's advice: Follow your heart, believe in
fate and never give up hope of finding true love.
And use a helpful hint from Fausto and always
remember to throw your coins with your left hand!*

Made in the USA
San Bernardino, CA
08 June 2014